# A COMMENTARY ON THE GOSPEL OF THOMAS

By Reverend Dr. Albert Gani

# A Commentary on the Gospel of Thomas
### Reverend Dr. Albert Gani

Published by:
The Church of the Path, Inc.
207 S. Commons Ford Road, Austin, Texas 78733 U.S.A.
(512) 263-9435 | contact@churchofthepath.org
www.churchofthepath.org

All rights reserved. No part of this book may be reproduced or transmitted in any form or by any means, electronic or mechanical, including photocopying, recording or by any informational storage or retrieval system without written permission from the author, except for the inclusion of brief quotations in a review.

Copyright © 1994 and 2022 by The Church of the Path®

ISBN-13: 978-1-882853-33-5

Excerpts from THE SECRET BOOKS OF THE EGYPTIAN GNOSTICS: AN INTRODUCTION TO THE GNOSTIC COPTIC MANUSCRIPTS DISCOVERED AT CHENOBOSKION by Jean Doresse, translated by Philip Mairet, copyright © 1958, 1959 by Librairie Plon; translation copyright © 1960, renewed © 1988 by Hollis & Carter, Ltd.. Used by permission of Viking Books, an imprint of Penguin Publishing Group, a division of Penguin Random House LLC. All rights reserved.

Cover Image: Saint Thomas the Apostle Tiffany Glass. Old Blandford Church, Petersburg, Virginia. Image courtesy of Library of Virginia.

# DEDICATION

**To the Christ and the Hierarchy,**
Whose strong presence is to be felt in the giving of the new dispensation and in the momentous events of the last quarter of this century.

# ACKNOWLEDGMENTS

First and foremost, immense gratitude goes from me to Curtis Jordan for his tireless transcriptions and corrections of my dictation, and for typesetting as well. Many thanks also to Rev. Dr. Robin Gani, Debra McClure, Siobhan McKillop, and Ronnie Baker for editing.

## WARNING - DISCLAIMER

This book is an invitation to spiritual introspection. It is sold with the understanding that it, or anyone involved in publishing or marketing it, make no claims of healing of any kind.

The purpose of this book is to inspire you to spiritual and ethical life. The author or anyone else involved in publishing or marketing it will not have any liability and desist themselves of any responsibility to any person or group or company for any damage or loss incurred in any way by the contents of this book.

# GLOSSARY

**Crucifixion of the Ego:** The process of crucifying the false self (the little ego) in order to reunite with the Greater Ego (the Higher Self).

**Divine Self:** See "Higher Self and Lower Self"

**Distorted Self:** See "Higher Self and Lower Self"

**Evil:** Anything that impairs progress. Any hindering factor, whether in thought, feeling, word, action, or non-action. Any denial of truth.

**Forces of Light:** Forces of God—goodness, beauty, truth.

**Forces of Darkness:** Forces of evil—deception, untruth, involution.

**Freezes:** Decelerated, petrified, crystallized truth; also known as "images." An image is an incomplete perception of a reality. Therefore, it always is a misconception and a presumption.

**Glamour:** An exaggeration of a divine aspect or attribute. For example, the glamour of strength leads to brutality and cruelty; the glamour of love leads to lack of discipline and permissiveness; the glamour of intelligence leads to inaction, and so forth.

**Hierarchy, The:** The Hierarchy is an organization formed by superhumans, some of whom never incarnated on Earth, and some who have but who have ascended to be masters. The departments of this organization are representatives of the Seven Rays. At the head of each one of these departments is a master who dispenses to humanity that which it is ready to assimilate.

**Higher Self and Lower Self:** The Higher Self is connected to the Divine. It is the best in us, our nucleus. It can also be seen as infinite, i.e., not just the nucleus but everything about us. The lower self is the undeveloped part of the self. It starts within us as potentiality. Wrongly activated these potentialities become harmful, creating our harmfulness. The task of life is to take responsibility for the lower self, having it join the Higher Self (see below for idealized self).

**Idealized Self:** A term abundantly and wonderfully used by Karen Horney. It covers up the lower self, presenting the "right" image. A person may have many idealized selves, or many idealized images in one idealized self. I put on a particular idealized self when I am in a high society cocktail party, another when I am at home with my wife and children, another when I'm by myself, and so on. Many images of myself converge to create that idealized self, which I try to maintain. At some point in my life I become my idealized self, being disconnected, alienated, and increasing my anxiety. This creates identity problems. The idealized self has also been called "phony self" or "false self" or "pretentious self" or the "mask" or the "idolized self".

**Idolized Self:** See "Idealized Self"

**Image:** See "Freeze"

**Lower Self:** See "Higher Self and Lower Self"

**Mask:** See "Idealized Self"

**Mother-Father Split:** Inner duality and misconceptions based on parents or substitute parents. See the book *Know Thyself* by Rev. Dr. Albert Gani for an in-depth explanation.

**Plan of Salvation:** Universal plan of in which every entity participates leading back to unification with God.

**Rays of Aspect:** The three Rays of Aspect are Will, Love, and Active Intelligence. They correspond to the Christian Trinity. The Hindus and the Buddhists have parallel concepts. Everything in creation contains the three Rays of Aspect. To the degree a thought, a feeling, an act, a word are balanced in the three Rays of Aspect, they are the truth. It provides for a good measuring tool, a yardstick, of ethics and truth. The harmful side of the three Rays of Aspect are Willfulness, Cowardice, and Conceit.

**Tibetan, The:** A Tibetan disciple whose writings were channeled by Alice A. Bailey in the early twentieth century.

# INTRODUCTION

The Gospel of Thomas is a collection of 118 sayings of the Christ as recorded by an individual named Thomas. We know that one of the disciples of the Christ was called Thomas. Some people also believe that Thomas was Jesus' brother, or even His twin; The word "thomas" seems to mean "twin." The transcriber of these saying could have been that man.

This text was discovered in several different sites. One of them was found about the turn of the twentieth century in the form of a Greek translation; another was written in Aramaic. It is the one on which we comment today. The original one discovered in Greek has served as a reference point to translators such as Jean Doresse and others later.

The purpose of this book is not to delve into the archaeological significance of these manuscripts, but to examine and explain their esoteric meanings in order to obtain the full spiritual benefit of this much underrated and forgotten gospel.

Christ, Himself, taught belief systems that do not at all correspond to those of conventional religion. In many of its sayings, the Gospel of Thomas resembles accepted conventional versions of the Bible. However, as you will read, many of these sayings as they now appear in the Bible have been edited to make them palatable, thus diluting or entirely negating their spiritual value. The diluted words of the Bible are further watered down by conventional religion which interprets them to suit its own purposes.

Christ's words as conveyed in the Gospel of Thomas come very close to the teachings of The Church of the Path®.

Our intent in writing this book is to demonstrate that our beliefs are deeply rooted in early Christianity, the only valid Christianity, unadulterated by time, translation, bigotry, mixture with paganism, and narrow-mindedness.

At The Church of the Path we believe that all religions start with a positive essence. It is this essence that we seek continuously within ourselves and in the world around us. We also practice the process of self-transformation, the process of purification. It involves the search for the beam in our own eye before blaming others or outer circumstances for what is happening in our lives.

How have we created the situations in which we find ourselves? To find the answer, we must look in our unconscious. The formation of our unconscious starts primarily with the soul. It is the soul that releases into the personality material and conditions that then attract events on the outer level.

In psychology, it is believed that a person is a product of his experiences; he is shaped by stimuli to which he responds. We believe exactly the opposite: we stimulate the world; we create the world we live in, the conditions, events and circumstances of our lives. We attract the people around us. What is inside us is what draws to us that which is outside us and not the other way around. We create our own reality.

We believe that this is the only way to understand the world. Any other view would take away our power to change the universe or ourselves. We say that if you are looking for reasons for your happiness and unhappiness, you must look within yourself and with yourself only.

Establishing the connection between an inner state and an outer condition brings great relief. If you experience how you have created it, you are suddenly filled with the joy of being able to uncreate it.

God does exist; He is just. He has created the Law of Cause and Effect. It is up to us to find Him within us by reconnecting with our freedom of choice and how we have exercised it.

At The Church of the Path we believe, as did the early Christians, that you are the master of your own destiny. This is abundantly demonstrated time and again in the Gospel of Thomas. For many reasons, the passages that confirm this principle were removed from the accepted Gospels that now constitute the New Testament.

In the first place, it is not a very popular concept. No one wants to give up their "option" to blame others for what is happening to them. Furthermore, a religion that promises salvation without earning it becomes very attractive indeed since there is no work required to reach paradise; and, in fact, these religions discourage or prohibit such activities.

In addition to this, the church-established shepherds have a lot more power over their flock if they tell them that they are really not responsible for their own sins and that a Saviour is going to take away any and all of the consequences of those sins just as long as they pronounce His name and say they "believe."

Thus, the established churches became successful businesses by living off of everyone's despair while offering temporary, but very expensive, reassurance.

A manifestation of this on a smaller scale can be found in the selling of indulgences in the Middle Ages and early Renaissance. Indeed, the pope had them printed with his name on them. For the cost of a dispensation, you could have one sin absolved. The greater the sin, the greater the cost. Also, the richer you were, the more you paid for dispensations. The great beneficiary of the discovery of the printing press was, of course, the Catholic Church, since indulgences could now be mechanically turned out by the hundreds of thousands and sold throughout the Catholic world.

This outrage was finally challenged by a courageous member of the Catholic Church named Martin Luther. His success created two currents:

1. The Reformation, the new Protestant religion which drew itself closer to the Law of Cause and Effect, the Law of Personal Responsibility. Indeed, according to the Protestant work ethic you worked and, as a result of your efforts, you earned money.

This belief formed the basis of the Age of Reason as well as of the Industrial Revolution—it is at the base of the success of the West. It propelled non-Catholic countries such as England, Holland and some parts of what is called today Germany to greater and greater wealth and success to the detriment of such countries as France, Spain and Italy which maintained their Catholicism.

2. As a reaction to this came the Counter-Reformation, mainly as a result of the thrust created by Ignatius of Loyola who initiated the Jesuit order. The Jesuits took the responsibility of educating the Catholic Church and making it more attractive to its participants, i.e., opening it up to the world. They had to find a way to explain progress in Catholic terms—an impossible task.

To compensate for this, the Catholic Church engaged in an orgy of baroque and rococo ornaments in their churches. There is not one cathedral in Europe that has not been modified by extraordinarily elaborate—and out of place—sculpture and paintings of the seventeenth and eighteenth centuries which grossly clash with the Gothic simplicity of those magnificent edifices. In fact, this is not just something that we denounce. It is denounced in the Catholic Church itself.

When I visited Citeux, an abbey which existed since early Middle Ages, it was clear that the monks there did not like what the Catholic Church tried to do in the seventeenth and eighteenth centuries to attract more participants. What a show!

I am not saying that the Jesuits brought about the rococo ornamentation. What I am saying is that the Jesuit attempt at reconciling the scientific and philosophic progress of humanity during the Renaissance with the already outdated Catholic creed did not work.

As a result, and in order to increase a lagging church attendance and retrieve some of the congregation attracted to Protestant religions, a lot of artificial means were used. Rococo and baroque ornamentation are not the only artifices employed.

For example, the close alliance of the clergy with the nobility during those centuries was another ploy. The church made sure that a co-dependent relationship was established between its high clergy and the nobility. Noble families bought cardinalates and bishoprics for what was usually the third son in the family. At some point, one could find cardinals in their teens and popes who had never been in the order.

None of this would have happened in the Catholic Church had the Law of Personal Responsibility been practiced. None of this is possible if accountability becomes part of anybody's creed. Corruption starts the minute personal responsibility and accountability are forgotten.

Many New Age teachings are actually reincarnations of early Christian teachings—as well as eastern teachings, of course. At The Church of the Path, we do not believe in all of the New Age teachings. Nor did the followers of Thomas obviously believe in all of Gnosticism with its totally unnecessary and very complicated universal and hierarchical systems. For example, from our point of view, we see magical thinking and unreality in conventional religion, in Gnosticism, and in many New Age teachings. Although we choose not to believe in magical thinking, we do not prevent those who do from attending our church services or from being members of our church. We say, "believe what you experience and gently discard the rest without condemning it."

The 118 sayings in the Gospel of Thomas are preceded by these words of the Christ: **"Whoever penetrates the meaning of these words will not taste death!"** Fear of death is fear of life. Conquering the fear of death automatically brings us to self-actualization. The whole point of our existence on Earth is the conquest of the fear of death. In reality, there is no death; the death that we experience is the death of the body.

An understanding of these teachings of the Christ will begin to liberate us from the fear of death. Incorporation of these lessons into the fabric of our life will bring us to self-actualization and the complete accomplishment of our task. It is obvious that study of these sayings is of paramount importance to anyone interested in self-actualization.

Enjoy, and apply them to your personal life!

# NUMBER ONE

*Jesus says: "Let him who seeks cease not to seek until he finds: when he finds he will be astonished; and when he is astonished he will wonder, and will reign over the universe!"*

Your birthright is the state of at-onement with God, which is the state of total grace. This state has no compromise; it knows no relative levels; it is absolute and it is one. Any area of your life in which you are not in total grace and ecstasy reveals self-created problems. Therefore, these areas constitute an invitation to seek. So, this saying addresses the necessity to remain on a specific problem until it transforms itself into complete and total resolution.

Is this, then, perfectionism? We must distinguish between perfectionism and seeking perfection. Perfectionism demands perfection *now* without effort. Seeking perfection accepts process, effort; it accepts the present conditions while continuing to strive. Perfectionism is a closed energy system. It is heavy. Striving for perfection is an open system that pursues the Absolute while at the same time accepting the relative state. Being an open system, it makes itself available to ever-increasingly satisfying experiences. An open person who seeks perfection will indeed be "astonished" continuously. He will continue to discover over and over again.

This state of continuous openness and wonder and astonishment will exist in an individual who has a good balance of all his expressive powers (such as the ability to think, feel, emote, give and take) and who has allowed his instincts to reach their divine consummation.

The five instincts and their divine consummation are as follows:

1) The Instinct of Self-Preservation—when allowed to reach the point where the individual is conscious of immortality, then he is indeed astonished, he indeed wonders and he reigns over the universe.

2) The Instinct of Procreation is consummated in the experience of merging with God, since the divine consummation of procreation is religion.

3) The Herd Instinct brings us to civilization.

4) The Instinct of Self-Assertion consummates itself in self-actualization.

5) However, it is in the final instinct, the Instinct of Enquiry, that this saying finds its best meaning. The Instinct of Enquiry is what we so often see unadulterated in children in their desire to know, hunger to learn. The consummation of this thirst and wonderment is knowledge; and knowledge leads to wisdom. Having wisdom is akin to reigning over the universe.

\*\*\*

We can also relate this saying to mastery. "*Let him who seeks cease not to seek*" means that one has to take a patient step-by-step approach to the resolution of a problem or to the acquisition of a skill. "*When he finds, he will be astonished*" corresponds to the response from the Universal Life Force which comes in and meets one's effort with reward.

One can discover this reality whenever one tries to acquire a skill. In the beginning, there is a lot of fumbling and mistakes. The person must take repeated risks on a very conscious level before the skill is mastered. Initially, there are occasional glimpses of what it would be like to be able to walk or to swim or to ride a bicycle.

After a while, the ability gels and becomes permanent. Then, as if by magic, the person realizes that he can swim or ride a bicycle or play the piano. The astonishment translates itself into a feeling of being on top of the world, reigning over the universe.

# NUMBER TWO

*Jesus says: "If those who seek to attract you say to you: 'See, the Kingdom is in heaven!' then the birds of heaven will be there before you. If they say to you: 'It is in the sea!' then the fish will be there before you. But the kingdom is within you and it is outside of you!"*

In this early Christian papyrus we find Christ admonishing people about seeing God as being up there in the sky or down there under the sea. This saying demonstrates that early Christianity was a lot more concerned with the inner kingdom of God than is modern Christianity. Indeed, present-day Christianity has degenerated into seeking God on the outside, in heaven or elsewhere; the church does not suggest looking for Him where He resides.

Consider, then, this proposal from the Christ—the invitation to look for God inside. Let no one ever say that seeking of God within started with the New Age or was a product of eastern philosophy, etc. Here it is in Christ's own words: do not look for God anywhere else *but within yourself*.

God—the answer to all our questions, the state of grace, infinite and omnipotent—is within us. Being within us, He certainly is within our reach. He is more within our reach than anything else in the universe, and, therefore, self-transformation is very much the road to God. However, only if I transform myself will I be able to find Him within myself. In spite of the lip service conventional Christianity pays to seeking God within, no such thing is taught or even encouraged, and, in fact, followers are required to seek God only as dictated by the religious organization. According to conventional Christianity, it is impossible to explain why certain things happen to us. I once told a Presbyterian minister that he created his own reality. "It rains on everybody," was his rebuttal.

In order to find God within you, what do you have to do? You merely have to remove the barriers that have prevented you from finding Him there. You have taken yourself away from God, away from the consciousness that God inhabits you right here and now, away from the Universal Life Force that created you. To a great extent, you have made your life the enemy of God within you.

And there is more to this saying. In comparing the seekers of God in heaven to birds, the Christ gives us quite a bit to ponder on. The birds who will find God before we do have the ability to fly; we cannot fly. This means that no specific outer level skill is necessary or required to find God within. It is a question of *unlearning* and going to the source that will bring us to God.

There is also something else here. How many people around you are not serious about seeking God; they take it lightly, as if they were birds? I call them spiritual butterflies. They flutter busily from workshop to workshop, from discipline to discipline. They seek on the outside that to which they are blind within themselves. What dark side of yourself are you trying to escape by becoming a bird fluttering from one line of study to another?

If God is up there in heaven, does that not also perpetuate the fallacy of seeing yourself as *merely* a miserable sinner and, therefore, as incapable of doing anything about your life? This is a favourite distortion of conventional Christianity—that you can really change very little about yourself, that you are a worthless sinner, that you will die, and on Judgment Day the determining factor as to whether or not you will make it to Paradise will be whether you believed or not that Christ vicariously "saved" you.

What about the fishes? Here the Christ is warning us of the exact opposite distortion to the one found in conventional Christianity. In conventional Christianity, God is sought in the sky, as a transcendent entity.

In paganism, even in Gnosticism, God is underwater, God is unconscious. Being underwater is a symbol of the unconscious. What is referred to here is the magical thinking that says we do not have to develop, we do not have to purify, we do not have to do anything, that nature will take care of us all by itself. This, of course, unleashed the license that we experienced in the 1960s and 1970s which contained all of the excesses and barbarities of paganism.

If sought within oneself, God will appear to blend the two. He will be seen as immanent and transcendent—inside and outside. He will be seen everywhere. The requirement, of course, is first to find Him within yourself.

# NUMBER THREE

*"When you know yourselves, then you will be known, and you will know that it is you who are the sons of the living Father. But if you do not know yourselves, then you will be in a state of poverty, and it is you [who will be] the poverty!"*

Once again the focus is on knowing yourself. Total self-knowledge is total self-actualization, and therefore, total atonement with God. To the degree one knows one's self, to that degree one is at-one with God and has accomplished one's task. We stress self-knowledge as a fundamental prerequisite and as a continuous endeavour. In saying this, the Christ joins Socrates: Know Thyself. It is amazing that the later developments of the church totally precluded this whole focus on self-knowledge and replaced it with outer level superstitions, rituals and dogmas.

Furthermore, when you know yourself, *"then you will be known."* When you know yourself, you reveal your Real Self. People will then **know** you for the first time. Until you know yourself, people do not know who you are—they know who you pretend to be; they know what you do to receive approval.

When you finally destroy all of your falsehoods, all of your masks and all of your pretenses, your Real Self will be revealed and then you will be known for who you really are. You will also be known by God. God cannot communicate to you through the mazes of pretenses, of masks, of idealizations, of lies, of demands, of denials, of conceit and of self-depreciation. When you get to know yourself, or **as** you get to know yourself, you will know God. You will know that you know God and you will know that He knows you.

*"And you will know that it is you who are the sons of the living Father."* Knowing yourself is achieving sonship. That state is already in you. It is only a question of discovering it and identifying with it. Here again, the Christ is telling us that He is not the only son of God, that every single person is a son of God and that every single person has God within him and has within him the potential of Godhood. Without this hope and without this goal, there is no point to life. So, far from being heresy, the attempt to at-one with God, the attempt to identify oneself with God is the highest possible pursuit.

We see also here an answer to the problem of fear. Fear is a direct product of numbing, of creating an unconscious. We are afraid of the unknown. We are, therefore, afraid of ourselves and of the projections of ourselves. The elimination of the unconscious eliminates fear entirely, because once the unknown becomes known, there is nothing to fear. With the elimination of fear, death disappears and eternal life becomes a reality.

The second part of the saying considers what happens by not knowing ourselves. What is created then is a state of poverty. Poverty, as we will see later, cannot possibly be idealized. We are not here talking about poverty on the material or on the financial levels, although that is also possible as a consequence of poverty on the other levels. We are talking about poverty on the other levels—the poverty that comes from superstition, narrow mindedness, fear, conceit, self will, etc.

*"And it is you who will be the poverty,"* describes the state of identification with lack. You are in a state of poverty consciousness; you are destitute. The opposite state,

wherein you know yourself, is a state of infinite abundance; in that state, there is no lack or poverty, no matter what the circumstances and events on the outer level may be.

# NUMBER FOUR

*Jesus says: "Let the old man heavy with days hesitate not to ask the little child of seven days about the Place of Life, and he will live! For it will be seen that many of the first will be last, and they will become a [single thing!"]*

The old man heavy with days is suffering from an accumulation of wrong knowledge, wrong conclusions, bad habits, misinterpreted truths, etc. The little child of seven days is a symbol of the innocent and primary knowledge of the Seven Rays of Aspect and Attribute.

For the sake of the reader's edification, there are three major Rays of Aspect—the First Ray of the Father (the Ray of Will), the Second Ray of the Son (the Ray of Love and Wisdom), and the Third Ray of the Mother (the Ray of Active Intelligence and Adaptability). These correspond to the Trinity. There are also four minor Rays—the Fourth Ray of Harmony through Conflict, the Fifth Ray of Concrete Knowledge through Science, the Sixth Ray of Idealism and Devotion, and the Seventh Ray of Order, Ceremony and Magic. All of the universe's creations can be divided or seen through the knowledge of these Seven Rays.

The Christ is referring here to the fact that a child has to have lived at least seven days to know anything, i.e., one must have experienced the Seven Rays in their original form without distortion or glamorization in order to fully know about the "Place of Life." (The "Place of Life" means the place of eternal life—at-onement with God.) Is anyone able to perfectly do that? The answer is an emphatic "no."

The fundamental problem of being born in this three-dimensional reality is that we have to undergo a period of time during which our primitive self must be contained, must be given limits in order to allow the real conscience to emerge. As much as this is necessary, it has an unfortunate result—the repression of the primitive self and the ensuring of guilt for that repression. As an adult, we have enough consciousness to accept and reveal our primitive self in its undeveloped state, to give it consciousness so it can grow to its full potential.

Did the Christ undergo this process? Or, was He perfect at birth? We believe that He did undergo this process, that He was *not* perfect at birth. He underwent the human experience of being born with a primitive self followed by the gradual rediscovery of that primitive self and through it the discovery of the Higher Self. For the Christ, this happened when His time had come. The ministry at the end of His life is a time when He had achieved the self-actualization that comes when the expression of the Seven Rays returns to its original purity. He transcended death. If the old man has the courage and the honesty to integrate the child of seven days with its innocent and primary knowledge, then he will live forever. He will have transcended death.

There is another meaning to this which emerges from a discovery that I made in 1976 concerning people's interests and directions. This is described in great detail in my book, *Know Thyself*. However, for the sake of clarity I will explain briefly what my discovery was.

It seems that a person goes through phases in life during which he changes his personality type, his Ray type, his characterology. The characterology which he had before puberty is reversed at, or through, puberty and returns at the time of menopause (age 42 to 55). For example, a person having a particular function, say Function A, from age 0 to puberty, changes to Function B at puberty and then returns to Function A at menopause.

Here it is! The old man making contact with the little child. The whole mystery of life can be resolved if childhood is understood and integrated, if and when all of the unconscious material is illuminated.

Why is it so very important for all of the unconscious to be illuminated? First, let's go back to the formation of the unconscious. As explained above, the process of disciplining and containing the primitive self is a necessary process. Unfortunately, in doing this one creates guilt for that primitive self. One becomes more and more ashamed of the primitive self as a result of that guilt combined with the demands we make upon ourselves. The weight of the guilt and the shame results in repression. The primitive self and all that can possibly be reminiscent of it become repressed and create the unconscious.

However, the story does not end there. All soul movements come through the primitive self. If the primitive self is repressed and lives in the unconscious, then all soul movement comes from the unconscious as an underground wave that must find expression, often volcanically, through what has been superimposed on top of it.

The little conscious self does not know and does not want to know that a lot of its actions are motivated by the unconscious. It is simultaneously disconnected from it and spellbound by it. That is why on the one hand we often feel victimized by the urges that we experience inside which seem to be irrepressible, and on the other hand victimized by events that happen to us which seem outside of our control. In actuality, both the urges that come from within and the events coming from without have their origin in what has been repressed within ourselves. This is the little child of seven days who experiences the Seven Rays in their primitive state.

The old man heavy with days is the world-weary individual who has not, as yet, been able to take responsibility for what is happening to him, both on the inside and on the outside. The little child is closer to the place of life than is the old man. The little child with his primitive purity when combined with the old man's experience, developed consciousness and wisdom will revive the old man *"and he will live!"*

*"The first will be last"* is demonstrated in the cycle I just described: that which was first experienced in our lives is experienced again at the end of our lives.

*"And they will become a single thing"* means that there will be unification; the person will be at-one with himself again. Functions A and B will be forever blended, and in this unification the person will become at-one with God.

I would like to say here to all of the people in psychology, psychiatry, psychotherapy and psychoanalysis that in no way should they consider themselves to be the inventors of the whole business of delving into childhood, and of remembering and illuminating the unconscious. This is a spiritual practice. It was a spiritual practice long before Mr. Freud and his atheism came to exist. Therefore, it is absurd for these professions to try to regulate the process of healing souls, or to know souls. Psychology, the knowledge of the soul, is first and foremost a spiritual endeavour. It was and will remain a spiritual endeavour long after the practice of psychology will have been abandoned. There is no possible practice of psychology without the acceptance of the search for God. It makes absolutely no sense. The entire pursuit of healing must be the seeking of a "single thing," becoming at-one with the self.

"*Let the old man heavy with days hesitate not to ask the little child of seven days about the Place of Life.*" This legitimizes faith, religion and the pursuit of God as the ultimate psychological healer, and the only true healer.

# NUMBER FIVE

*Jesus says: "Know what is before your face, and what is hidden from you will be revealed to you. For nothing hidden will fail to be revealed!"*

Here the Christ is telling us that if we will only take the trouble of becoming aware of what is in front of us, of what is before our face, our problems will be resolved through the rediscovery of what is unconscious.

You need not go any further than looking at what is before your face. If you consciously put an honest effort into dealing with what is before you, with what comes to you, with what you are aware of, then *"what is hidden from you will be revealed to you."*

This means that if you really have done the work on the outer level as much as you possibly could, then everything else will fall into place. The unconscious will join you; it does not have to be forced, you do not have to effect tours de force on yourself in order for that to occur. It will come and join you effortlessly.

You can see that many shortcuts have been developed which are regressive. Take hypnotism as an example. It has become a way of bypassing the necessity of doing the job of illuminating yourself. It is an easy way to be "fixed" while not doing the work or taking responsibility for your own progress.

*"For nothing hidden will fail to be revealed."* All secrets will be shouted from rooftops. A secret wants to reveal itself. A secret cannot remain secret forever no matter how hard you try. It will kill you.

To what extent do you keep secrets; to what extent do you lie; to what extent do you pretend? To that extent you are dualizing yourself, splitting yourself in two, tearing yourself apart. It is no use hiding; it is very much to your detriment. It is a lot more in your best interest to tell the truth because the truth will bring lasting success. Lies may bring instant and temporary success, but calamity and destruction will follow.

# NUMBER SIX

*His disciples asked and said to him: "Do you want us to fast? How shall we pray, how shall we give alms, what rules concerning eating shall we follow?" Jesus says: "Tell no lie, and whatever you hate, do not do: for all these things are manifest to the face of heaven; nothing hidden will fail to be revealed, and nothing disguised will fail before long to be made public!"*

What an indictment of all of the nonsensical empty rituals and superstitions to be found in every accepted conventional religion! Clearly the Christ says here, it is not whether you fast, or how much you give alms, or what you eat or do not eat that counts. What counts is that you be in truth, that you do your task.

He reminds us again that everything is known to heaven, i.e., to God, and that nothing hidden will fail to be revealed.

This is happening in our day. Hypocrisy is becoming less and less possible. In the past, presidents were allowed to be much more licentious and self-indulgent than they are today. Indeed, there was no public outcry against their mistresses or their gross obesity. The close scrutiny now imposed upon those running for political office is a manifestation of the incoming Christ. His closeness to our level results in this urge to purge. There is less and less to hide.

Modern technology is making it less and less possible to have secrets. Cause is getting closer and closer to effect. This is a manifestation of progress, of acceleration. Far from curtailing our freedoms, this increases our freedoms, for there is no freedom without responsibility.

The same technology which makes it impossible for us to cheat enables us to live in infinitely better conditions than ever before. The fact that anything happening anywhere on Earth can be transmitted within minutes to anybody on Earth is a direct out-picturing of the incoming Christ energy. If Christ's disciples could glimpse the way we live today, this is what they would say. They would see in our way of life the precise confirmation of what they were taught by their Master.

What about *"and whatever you hate, do not do"*? If we are not to do what we hate, then we are to do what we love. This points to the fact that the accomplishment of our task is pleasurable. Doing it is pleasurable. Movement is pleasurable. Being in truth is pleasurable.

This saying can easily be misinterpreted as an invitation to the line of least resistance, i.e., if you don't like it, don't do it. On the contrary, the Christ is saying that we should take care of our unpleasant tasks. Not doing what needs to be done is hateful and hostile.

From the Higher Self's point of view, everything needing to be done is pleasurable. For example, how pleasurable is it to "tell no lie"? To the degree you find that painful, to that degree you are still a liar and doing what you hate. You are not in the position to totally enjoy and inhabit your task. Let that be a test to you. The ease with which you can live in total truth corresponds to the joy and pleasure with which you accomplish your task.

# NUMBER SEVEN

*Jesus says: "Blessed is the lion which a man eats so that the lion becomes a man. But cursed is the man whom a lion eats so that the man becomes a lion!"*

The man eating the lion (the superior being eating the inferior being) is blessed. We must "eat" our lower self, i.e., integrate it, digest it, assimilate it, convert its energy, metabolize and funnel it into the positive purpose of our consciousness. The reverse is a perversion. There is regression when the lion eats the man and the man becomes the lion. Consciousness is then put to the service of the lower self. The lower nature becomes the ruler of consciousness which is then disconnected from the Universal Life Force.

When we lose faith, we are in the process of being devoured by our lower selves. The type of thinking and, therefore, of feeling and action, of the person who is faithless is regressive and dangerous. What he rationalizes is fundamentally evil since the originator is the lion and the man its slave.

On the Path, we look for our freezes. We call freezes those wrong conclusions that were reached very early in life which we then continue to perpetuate and which create so much havoc in our lives. For example, if my mother was withholding and I concluded that all women are withholding, the equation: *women = withholding* is a freeze. Later, I will build an entire lifestyle based on this wrong conclusion. I am, therefore, ruled by the wrong opinion. I am "eaten" by this lion, by this inferior entity within me. Freezes have an

Instinct of Self-Preservation. They want to perpetuate themselves. They also want to accelerate the process of self-perpetuation which brings us to crisis.

As long as I do not want to resolve my freeze which says that women are withholding, any attempt at having a relationship or improving an existing relationship will be futile since it would serve the purpose of feeding that lion. The only result will be unhappiness and destruction.

On a global level we can find the same type of situation. If we examine fascism, for example, we will see that it is based on wrong premises, wrong thinking. Any advance or progress achieved by fascism merely went to feeding the lion. The lion had to be annihilated completely before the countries it had devoured could find new life, this time based on consciousness—on the man eating the lion not on the lion eating the man.

When a beast is mortally wounded it is the most dangerous. When our lower self, the lion in us, the freezes within us, is revealed and confronted, it wages its most ferocious battle. This same principle is found in the concept of the Dweller on the Threshold. When a person is close to initiation, i.e., when his lower self is mortally wounded, it manifests more powerfully than ever as the one entity which prevents him from going past the door of initiation. This test must be successfully undergone before the person can be invested with more powers, more energies, more consciousness.

# NUMBER EIGHT

*Then he says: "A man is like a skilled fisherman who cast his net into the sea. He brought it up out of the sea full of little fishes, and among them the skilled fisherman found one that was big and excellent. He threw all the little fishes back into the sea; without hesitating he chose the big fish. He who has ears to hear, let him hear!"*

Development of the inner ear is needed to understand this saying. It refers to our spiritual search. In the process of it, we are like fishermen, casting our nets, i.e., being open to any and all teachings. What we find in our nets is a smorgasbord of them all. It is up to us to recognize the one fish that is big and excellent, i.e., the one absolute teaching, the truth. We find it in the midst of all the little half-truths that have not as yet become big and that need to be thrown back into the sea to develop.

From the point of view of the relative versus the Absolute, the Christ is inviting us to choose only the one Absolute. Sometimes the "big fish" can be found amongst many little fishes in one set of teachings.

A good example of this practice is our approach to the teachings of the Tibetan, as given through Alice Bailey, and the teachings of *The Urantia Book*. We take from these works what corresponds to the Absolute, what makes sense with the ultimate philosophy, the Greatest Life. The search for the Absolute over the relative can also be found in philosophy, outside of the "spiritual."

Hegel, for example, was always in search of the Absolute. His philosophy, as well as all of the wonderful conclusions that he arrived at, always has for its base the Absolute and always returns to the Absolute.

Notice, also, that there is only one big fish. There is only one truth. There is only one teaching. There is only one God.

This **ONE** is found to be the essence of every single religion, every single body of knowledge, and every single philosophy. It is this essence that needs to be sought, not only outside of ourselves, but inside ourselves as well. Only experientially can it be found—experientially through the inner ear.

When you find the big fish, it is important to stay with it. Do not be a Jonah trying to escape your task. The "great fish," as described in the Bible in the story of Jonah, will seek you out, swallow you and throw you right back on the shores of your task.

This is an extremely important teaching for New Age spiritual butterflies—and there are many of them to be found fluttering about—tons of little fishes who go to other little fish teachers to be fed with nonsense.

# NUMBER NINE

*Jesus says: "See, the sower went out. He filled his hand and scattered [the seed.] Some fell on the path: birds came and gathered them. Others fell on rocky ground: they found no means of taking root in the soil and did not send up ears of corn. Others fell among thorns; [these] stifled the grain, and the worm ate the [seed.] Others fell on good soil, and this [portion] produced an excellent crop: it gave as much as sixty-fold, and [even] a hundred and twenty-fold!"*

The Christ speaks here to the process of scattering, of being open. This time the allegory takes us to a sower. He scatters the seed. We must scatter ourselves, squander ourselves on the universe, generously and totally. We must also broadcast and lavish our knowledge, the truth. Most of those scatterings will be for naught. For example, some will be eaten by birds.

Here, we have the sense of the Christ's annoyance at this type of person. It is, indeed, very frustrating to see people come in and out of our church, nibbling some of the seed without being grateful, and then, going away to nibble somewhere else, never taking in or committing to a discipline. It is a waste of time, theirs and ours.

*"Others fell on rocky ground, they found no means of taking root in the soil and did not send up ears of corn."* This refers to the people who have such a hard-core defense that the teaching bounces right off of them, never taking root, never developing into anything significant.

*"Others fell among thorns; these stifled the grain, and the worm ate the seed."* Here a reference is made to the forces

that suppress, kill, or obliterate the teachings. Any new dispensation has to undergo this type of treatment, since, by definition, it comes in to destroy the status quo and inaugurate a new era. The teachings of our church have been subjected to all of these treatments as mentioned here by the Christ.

"*Others fell on good soil, and this portion produced an excellent crop; it gave as much as sixty-fold, and even a hundred and twenty-fold.*" This, of course, refers to the fact that the very few seeds finding fertile soil are enough to multiply exponentially.

It only takes a few people to be receptive—good soil—to a set of teachings for them to be propagated into the rest of the earth. This was certainly true of the Christ, whose disciples were very few in the beginning. It was also true of Mohammed, whose teachings were listened to only by his wife, Hadija, and his friend, Abu-Bakr.

In spite of this scarcity of good soil, the crop will be excellent and will multiply. The sixty-fold and one hundred and twenty-fold refer to exponentiality, sixty-four being the sixth power of two and one-hundred-twenty-eight being the seventh.

# NUMBER TEN

*Jesus says: "I have cast a fire onto the world, and see, I watch over it until it blazes up!"*

New teachings have the property of fire. They burn down old, dried up and obsolete forms in order to create new ones. It is unfortunate that it has to be this way. The purer the new teachings, the more destructive will be the fire that they cast onto the world. That Christ is watching over it until it blazes up is an indication of His ever-presence while humanity integrates His teachings on deeper and deeper levels. He will be with us until the last person is saved.

I cannot help but reflect upon Nero's setting Rome and Alexandria on fire and enjoying the spectacle, giving as an excuse the fact that he wanted to build a new Rome in its place. This historical example, when pitted against this saying of Jesus highlights the fact that the forces of darkness continuously mirror the Forces of Light, only their intent is wrong and the outcome is disaster and death. The intent of the Forces of Light is always good and right and connected with the infinite; it perpetrates eternal life.

Each one of you has the potential of casting a fire onto your own world. If you have not done it yet, you have not lived. You have not apprehended your task. You are living the life of a coward, delaying the time when you will finally do what you have to do.

Setting your life on fire is stopping the compromise, reaching the point of relinquishing all of that which you have made yourself believe, all of the ways that you have sold out for momentary and immediate gain. Look hard, question your beliefs—all of them—including the ones that you find most precious. Divest yourself of that which is unnecessary; throw it into the great fire of truth.

Are you aware of this? Or, are you so immersed in your defenses that, not only have you lost the opportunity to see and follow the light, but you have also forgotten that this opportunity was ever offered to you? If this is the case, watch out because you will be set on fire by somebody else's task.

The task was offered to you and you looked the other way into the pseudo-safety of approval and conventionality. It is now given to someone who is a lot more courageous than you. Unfortunately, the way you will now rediscover these opportunities can only be through challenges, or even worse, crises.

# NUMBER ELEVEN

*Jesus says: "This heaven will pass away, and the heaven which is above it will pass: but those who are dead will not live, and those who live will not die!"*

Here the Christ is referring to the two last rounds in the career of humanity. *"This heaven will pass away"* refers to our present solar system, the one in which we live, the one in which we will continue to live for what the mystics estimate to be another several million years. This cycle is the one that sees God as love. The saviour for us during this cycle is a Second Ray saviour, a teacher of love.

The *"heaven which is above it"* and which will descend is the last round for humanity. The saviour for this next round is going to be a "will function" saviour coming from the center where the will of God is known. During that period the will aspect of God will be revealed and integrated.

*"But those who are dead will not live, and those who live will not die."* Those who are dead are those who are not setting the world on fire. They are dead because they conform, because they protect themselves, because they are too much the cowards to allow themselves to become seeds and be scattered all over the universe. They are too lazy to look for the one big fish and they are too greedy to let go of all the other little fishes. They will not live; they will remain in their defenses and will descend into spheres of existence which are lower than the human sphere.

By contrast, *"those who live will not die."* Those who live are those who set the world on fire. They are those who follow the one absolute truth, the one big fish. They are those who have the courage to scatter themselves all over the universe. They are those who are generous enough to relinquish the little fishes. They are those who honestly and courageously work on that which is the worst within themselves, trying to transform it and make it the best. They are the people on the Path of Self-Transformation and Self-Purification. Those are the ones who are alive and they will not die, they will find eternal life.

Where do you stand? Are you alive or dead? Come to life! Set on fire what is obsolete. Purify the worst in you and make it divine, thus following the Christ. You will then be alive. You will find life and once you have found it, you will not want to let go of it. It will propel you into eternal life.

# NUMBER TWELVE

*"Today you eat dead things and make them into something living: [but] when you will be in Light, what will you do then? For then you will become two instead of one; and when you become two, what will you do then?"*

The Christ here refers to two types of dualities: the lower and the higher. He is speaking to people who are still very caught in the lower duality. And He is also concerned about what is going to happen to them when they reach the higher duality because they will not know what to do. What will *you* do then?

The lower duality has a mixture of positive and negative on each of its two sides. For example, if you consider the aspects and attributes of your mother and your father, you will find positive and negative on both sides. Let's say, for instance, that your mother is loving, weak and artistic, while your father is disciplined, cruel and mathematical. You can see here the type of duality that is found in all of common humanity.

Every single person has his own duality. It is only a question of finding it. This is what is meant when the Christ says *"You eat dead things and make them into something living."* Eating dead things corresponds to conforming to the freezes (misconceptions) that you have absorbed from your mother and your father.

For example, in the particular case cited above, a person will be tempted to associate love with weakness, and precision with cruelty. These are misconceptions which will propel him into incredible misery throughout his life unless he resolves them by bringing them to light (consciousness).

If he decides not to resolve his dualities, he has eaten dead things and **not** made them into something living, in which case he has not completed his task which will open to him only after the resolution of his misconceptions.

If you are an orphan (lacking mother and/or father) you may ask how this applies to you. Again, I say that every single person has his own particular brand of duality. It is usually identified as mother or father. However, it could be a parent versus an institution, or it could be both parents on one side versus something else on the other.

For example, I worked with a German man whose parents were Nazis; he experienced both his parents as harsh, cruel, demanding, unloving and unaffectionate. At the same time, the school that he attended provided him with the love, the warmth and the attention that the Nazi parents did not give him.

Conversely, a Jewish person with whom I worked in Europe and who had gone through World War II had an equal and opposite kind of duality. He experienced his parents as loving, but weak and vulnerable—they both died in a train which was blown up by the Nazis while the whole family was trying to escape. Conversely, the whole world out there was Nazi—punishing, inclement, untrustworthy. He remained a survivor, always trying to sneak in a little bit of affection here and there wherever he could find it.

*"But when you will be in Light, what will you do then? For then you will become two instead of one."* The resolution of the lower duality brings about the higher one. For example, it is true that love is not weak and that precision is not cruel. The higher duality is the one in which the disciple now sees the clear difference between love, strength, intelligence,

knowledge, harmony, faith, and order; versus cruelty, self-will, inertia, fear, materialism, bondage, pride, confusion, blindness, disorder, anarchy, lack of faith. In the Light, this higher duality between good and evil becomes obvious. It propels the disciple into action.

"*What will you do then?*" In which camp will you go? This refers to the choice that the disciple has on the threshold of the third initiation: following the Forces of Light or following the forces of darkness. The resolution of the personal images presents us with one last struggle: are we going to devote all of those skills that we have mastered for the purposes of Light, or for the selfish egocentric purposes of darkness. What will **you** do then?

This is indeed a major decision that needs to be made at the threshold of that initiation. The Tibetan says that this is the first initiation as far as the Hierarchy is concerned. When the right decision is made at this particular point of resolution of the higher duality, the individual in question has made it into the ranks of the Hierarchy. He is now ready to serve the Plan of Salvation.

What does the Christ mean by saying, "for then you will become two instead of one?" Does that mean that in the lower duality we are at-one? This seems to contradict the whole goal of at-onement since the point of evolution from the lower to the higher duality is to bring us closer to at-onement with God.

There are two states of at-onement. One is before consciousness, i.e., before the first initiation when the individual is still in the throes of his animalistic ways. His freezes propel him into many life experiences which he does not question. He goes through his life not asking why things are happening, or why he is creating them. He does not relate cause and effect. In that sense he is at-one, just as the rabbit who is eaten by a wildcat is at-one. The rabbit lives in this lower level of acceptance; this is the state of being without awareness; consciousness has not arrived as yet.

When consciousness arrives, the person exists in a totally different state—the state of becoming. He is now consciously pursuing self-betterment. In a way, the state of becoming corresponds for ordinary humanity to the state of the higher dualism of the disciple where there is a conscious awareness of what is good and, by contrast, a conscious and deliberate desire to dissolve what is not.

What one is left with after reflecting upon this particular saying is the sense of frustration that the Christ must have experienced in trying to talk to people who were so very far away from His consciousness. What an enormous task, to try to put in understandable terms these huge philosophical concepts and teach them to people who were totally uneducated, as were His disciples.

He was not talking to philosophers, He was talking to very simple people. The advantage of talking to simple people is that they are not burdened by prior knowledge. The disadvantage is that they do not understand what you are saying. Therefore, the lessons have to be accessible to those primitive people and at the same time carry the eternal message which is still available for our benefit today.

# NUMBER THIRTEEN

*The disciples say to Jesus: "We know that Thou wilt leave us: who will [then] be the great[est] over us?" Jesus says to them: "Wherever you go, you will turn to James the Just, for whose sake heaven as well as earth was produced."*

The disciples here are very sad. This occurs when one knows that their teacher is dying. Where will I turn, who will be my authority after they leave?

If you have not found the "big fish", if you have not found your teacher, if you have not wanted to find your teacher, you will not know what is being described here and you will not have experienced what I am trying to tell you. One day, however, you will. And then you will find yourself asking yourself that question.

The answer is very simple. There will come a point when you must be tried; the knowledge that the teacher has given you will be tested. If you pass, you will become a teacher to people around you. Later in this gospel there is going to be more on this subject. You will see how the Christ responds to His disciples about the matter.

In this one, He says *"wherever you go, you will turn to James the Just, for whose sake heaven as well as earth was produced."* I do not know why He said that. However, what I want to know is where is Peter? Nothing here is said about "On this rock I build my church" or anything like that. Peter is not even mentioned, but James is. James was Jesus' brother.

What does that mean? Does He tell us to follow His brother? Is there here an indication that since Christ is our elder brother, we should follow our own innermost self?

# NUMBER FOURTEEN

*Jesus says to his disciples: "Compare me, and tell me whom I am like." Simon Peter says to him: "Thou art like a just angel!" Matthew says to him: "Thou art like a wise man and a philosopher!" Thomas says to him: "Master, my tongue cannot find words to say whom thou art like." Jesus says: "I am no longer thy master; for thou hast drunk, thou art inebriated from the bubbling spring which is mine and which I sent forth." Then he took him aside; he said three words to him. And when Thomas came back to his companions, they asked him: "What did Jesus say to thee?" And Thomas answered them: "If I tell you [a single] one of the words he said to me, you will take up stones and throw them at me, and fire will come out of the stones and consume you!"*

Here the Christ again guides us from the relative to the Absolute. When Peter compares Him to an angel that is not satisfactory. Angels are relative, they are finite. Besides, what does Peter know about angels? I also sense Peter's attempt to butter up his teacher, a ploy that the teacher immediately rejects. Matthew compares Him to a wise man and a philosopher. Here again, it is not satisfactory. Philosophy is not necessarily grounded in spirituality. It is also very limiting.

Let's pause for a second and study the contrast between what Peter says and what Matthew says. Indeed, we will find in that contrast religion versus philosophy—religion, *"thou art like an angel,"* versus philosophy, *"thou art like a wise man and a philosopher."* One has to remember that in those days there were great debates, sometimes culminating in violence between the Greeks and the Jews.

The Greeks were, of course, pro-philosophy while the Jews were pro-religion. The Greeks were more concerned with outer level reality while the Jews were concerned with inner level reality. The Greeks had gods that could be compared to humans in their limited and accessible behaviour. The Jews had a God about whom naught could be said. This great conflict was settled by the teachings of Jesus, and also by the teachings of the Neoplatonists who tried to bridge Greek philosophy with Christianity—by Plotinus whom I am convinced was the reincarnation of Plato.

The solution is found by Thomas: "*My tongue cannot find words to say whom thou art like.*" Indeed, it is absurd to compare Jesus to anything that can be visualized by the limited human mind. Human language cannot adequately describe truth and eternity. Furthermore, is it necessary to try to describe, or try to compare, or try to precipitate that which belongs to the world of the spiritual?

The recognition of this fact makes Thomas more evolved than the other disciples and that is why Jesus takes him aside and gives him three secret words. Jesus teaches Thomas on a level that cannot be understood by the other disciples. A lot of the esoteric material that is now available to us was not taught to common people. It is dangerous to teach material of this caliber to people who are not ready to receive it. In their hands, these words become offensive. People will reject and throw stones at those who have said them.

"*For I am no longer thy master, for thou hast drunk, thou art inebriated from the bubbling spring which is mine and which I sent forth."* When Thomas demonstrates his understanding of spiritual reality by saying that it cannot be put in words who is the Christ, he in effect becomes the equal to the Christ. And the Christ indeed confirms this by saying, I don't have anything more to teach you, I am no longer your master.

Thomas has lost himself (is inebriated) in the teachings of the Christ. When we are involved in learning from a Master, we feel this sense of inebriation. It is akin to, but it is not addiction. It is the thirst for the Universal Life Force. Once you have found it, you know you are home and you are totally and entirely devoted to it, as a drunk is devoted to his bottle. Here we see the humility of the Christ who says if you understand this then I have nothing to teach you, you are My equal.

This contradicts all of the notions of Christ as He is described by conventional religion. Christ is not unobtainable, Christ is not one with God, Christ is different from God, He is a son of God as we are sons of God. Christ, Himself, is in a process of attaining God and so are we.

Thomas, on his level, has found his process. He has surrendered on his level to his process of purification. This surrender and the fact that he is on this Path, no matter the level, means he is Christ's equal. A person who is less developed, but who is nevertheless on the Path, is the equal of a more developed person who is also on the Path.

An excellent student in first grade who totally devotes himself to his studies is the equal to an excellent student in university who is totally devoted to his studies. The student in the university no longer has anything to teach the student of the first grade when it comes to devotion to the process of studying, of being on the Path.

Let's follow the sequence that is suggested by Thomas here in his response to his companions.

1. *"If I tell you a single one of the words he said to me you will take up stones and throw them at me."* This reminds us of the usual rejection of very powerful sayings. The discovery of a startling truth always brings about a challenge to something that already exists. Obviously, any one of the words imparted by Jesus to Thomas would have contradicted many of the misconceptions that the disciples had at that time.

If you take into consideration the fact that they were Jewish, you will come to realize that many of the Jewish teachings had already been contradicted by the Christ. Obviously, what was told Thomas in private was even more contradictory, even more scandalous and outrageous in the eyes of the consciousness of the disciples, and would incite them to take up stones to throw at Thomas.

2. *"And fire will come out of the stones and consume you."* The act of rejecting the truth, throwing stones at the truth, boomerangs right back onto the person who is rejecting and consumes the person who has thrown the stones.

Take any example you wish. When the Catholic Church threw stones at Copernicus and Galileo, the Catholic Church was consumed by the very stones they threw. When the Viennese psychiatric association condemned Freud for his discoveries of childhood sexuality, it was burned by its own stones. When the Roman Empire persecuted the Christians, it was itself annihilated, and so forth. If you throw stones at the truth, it is those very stones that you throw that will consume you and set you on fire.

What are some of the things that you find outrageous

around you? What are those aspects or people or situations that are so very much abhorrent to you? This abhorrence, this insulting attitude, this attack that you are perpetrating on these aspects or people or thought patterns or religions will consume you. Obviously, you detest because you harbour within yourself elements that are precisely the same as the ones that you hate on the outer level. Those outer level people, situations or ideas merely remind you of the fact that the inner ones live inside you and that you are so afraid of them. Your greatest teachers are those things, people, situations that you abhor with such great intensity. If you open your mind to them and if you embrace them, you have solved the great puzzle of your life and you will have found your task.

Resist not "evil." You are consumed by the truth only because you resist it. Resisting it, you become "dead matter" and you are reduced to ashes by the truth which then burns. However, if you allow yourself to be enriched by the truth and you do not resist it, if you embrace it and you do not discard it, if you do not react to it negatively, but instead integrate it, then it refreshes you and you find in it the light of truth, not consuming flames, but eternal life, the light life of the phoenix that rises from the ashes.

# NUMBER FIFTEEN

*Jesus says to them: "When you fast, you will beget sin for yourselves; when you pray, you will be condemned; when you give alms, you will do evil to your souls! [But] when you enter any land and travel over the country, when you are welcomed eat what is put before you; those who are ill in those places, heal them. For what enters into your mouth will not defile you, but what comes out of your mouth, it is that which will defile you!"*

Here the Christ admonishes us against relying on religious practices for the purpose of doing the work of God, or purifying, or healing others. *"When you fast you will beget sin for yourselves"* goes exactly opposite to the Jewish requirement of fasting on Yom Kippur.

Yom Kippur is the second highest holiday in the Jewish religion—the first one being the Sabbath. Not fasting during Yom Kippur is for the Jews a great sin.

Here the Christ contradicts this entirely by saying when you fast, you will beget sin for yourselves. He is denouncing fasting for the sake of showing off religiously. He does the same about prayer in the next phrase, "when you pray you will be condemned." Indeed, it is not the act of fasting or of praying, but the *reason* you fast and the *reason* you pray that condemn you.

At The Church of the Path®, we believe that pleasure and its pursuit are no different from ethics, or truth, or responsibility. If a cleansing or a fast is needed, it is undertaken solely for medicinal purposes, not as a religious practice. Enjoyment of food is very much a part of the joy of life. The enjoyment of a food that may not necessarily be healthy is healing in and by itself, by the mere fact of your enjoyment of it.

When it comes to prayer, prayers in our Faith are quite different from the ones found in conventional religion. They do not ask that anything be granted that we have not earned. They ask for the courage and the honesty to pay the price for what we want. They ask for the fortitude and the openness to look within and be able to face all of the negativities and the impurities, all that of which we are ashamed and which also keeps us from everything that we can desire. Ultimately, every single wish will be fulfilled when it finds its original and instinctual expression within the context of consciousness.

*"When you give alms you will do evil to your souls."* This refers to false giving. Under what pretense do you give? If you give for glory, you are harming yourself and evil is done to your soul. Any alms which are received without being earned violate the Law of Cause and Effect and, therefore, encourage the evil of magical thinking.

The worst thing that can happen to an individual is to win the lottery when he is not ready to do so. The mere buying of a lottery ticket is breaking the Law of Cause and Effect and an attempt to get something for nothing, an attempt to get something that was not earned.

Does that mean that we should not help people? Does that mean that we should not assuage the pain and hunger of others? Does that make all welfare programs invalid? No, it does not. Welfare programs and helping people are very valid. Helping others is a requirement. However,

  (a) it has to be done selflessly, for the cause itself and for no other motive and

(b) it has to be done in such a way that it helps people help themselves. The minute a person has acquired the ways and means to help himself or herself, then we must stop the process of giving, or else giving will result in diminishing returns. Otherwise, it would reward the negative behaviour of not wanting to work and wanting to be a parasite on society. It is that parasitic aspect that is addressed here when the Christ says that giving alms does evil to souls.

\*\*\*

He then urges us to travel, to enter lands, to see the world and eat what is put before us. This encourages us to learn new things. We do not only eat with our mouths, we absorb through our eyes, through our ears, through our noses, through our brains, let alone the inner senses, of course. This is really an invitation not only to change, but to adapt to as many situations as exist in the world. This requires a great deal of humility as well as a freedom from the little ways and superstitions to which we are used to conforming. It is freedom from freezes, wrong conclusions, idealized selves, seeking approval, being the center of attention. It is the ability to give and to heal with whatever tools are found, wherever we happen to be. It is an invitation to translate eternal truths into every single language that exists, thereby healing those who are ill in those places.

\*\*\*

"For what enters into your mouth will not defile you." You cannot be hurt by anything you absorb. You can only be harmed if there is a weakness in you and you do not heal it. If you get exposed to a thing and it hurts you, that should be a demonstration of an area you must purify—this is true physically, emotionally and mentally.

How about all of the problems of freedom of speech? Can people, including children, be harmed by violence on television or sex on television? I believe that they can be harmed a lot more through violence on television than through sex on television.

However, sex is not allowed on television, but tons of violence is, with children watching people being dismembered in cartoons just about every day. When does a child see two beings making love? Why should that be censored? Isn't that a lot more natural than all of the cruelties that are being shown? No one can be hurt, including children, by exposure to anything.

On the contrary, the more the exposure, the greater the opportunity to understand and purify. Then the child, and later the adult, can make the choice of assimilating or not whatever he wants. He is prepared for having healthy reactions to anything he will encounter in life. "What enters you will not defile you."

"*But it is what comes out of your mouth, it is that which will defile you*" addresses that which needs to concern us. It is what we say, it is what we express, what we emanate that is harmful to us and to others. All of this is much more damaging than what we take in. The cultivation of harmlessness, which is purity of thought, feeling, action and word is what the Christ is urging us to do here—to watch what we say, to watch what we portray, what we represent, what kind of examples we offer others.

For example, somebody who is falsely religious and is exhibiting that in the presence of others is doing them great harm by influencing them in wrong directions, by distorting the nature of God and the nature of the universe for them. The price to pay is very dear for the person who does that and for the others who believe him.

# NUMBER SIXTEEN

*Jesus says: "When you see Him who has not been born of woman, bow down face to the earth and adore Him: He is your father!"*

Here the Christ is talking about God, not about Himself. God is not created. God creates. God initiates. He is not born out of any other being. He is masculine and feminine, man and woman.

However, there is more to say about this. Here is a key that will help you recognize a teacher, your teacher, teachings that you need to follow, lessons that you need to integrate. All of those have in common one thing—they are original, they are not born of anything, they are absolute, they are ultimately natural, they make infinite sense.

Sometimes one finds a teacher who is like this. Sometimes this purity is found in something a child says, or that a retarded person does. Sometimes it comes totally unexpectedly from somebody who is very negative or very evil. Regardless of its source, it is your job to recognize it and bow down to it and to do nothing else.

A lot of people recognize in what I say this aspect of originality, of the Absolute, of not being born of anything, of not being secondary to anything. I personally am not perfect. I am born of woman, but what I say, what I teach, what I try to portray is an attempt at being as close as possible to the Absolute, to the natural and to that which makes absolute sense. In that respect, I have followers. In that respect, then, many other teachers also have followers.

# NUMBER SEVENTEEN

*Jesus says: "Men indeed think I have come to bring peace to the world. But they do not know that I have come to bring to the world discord, fire, sword, war. Indeed, if there are five [people] in a house, they will become three against two and two against three—father against son and son against father—and they will be lifted up, being solitaries."*

This saying of the Christ corresponds to many others found in the other four gospels. It says basically: I did not come to bring you peace, I came to bring you the sword; I have come to set you at war against people you love and/or people who love you.

This is one of the most resisted sayings of the Christ because He reminds us that it is through conflict that harmony can be found. Conflict cannot be avoided if one is to find harmony. The process of numbing conflict through the pretense of love, pseudo-love, pseudo-peace, pseudo-knowledge, pseudo-indifference, is anti-life.

Instead, entering into conflict is the greatest spiritual endeavour that can be found because it will lift you up and make you a "solitary." What is meant by that is that it will raise you to the spiritual level and you will finally experience your uniqueness. There is no way you can experience your uniqueness unless you enter into conflict, especially the conflict that pits you against your parents. This is an extremely important element to take into consideration.

You cannot grow spiritually unless you undertake and dissolve and resolve the conflicts that exist between you and those who are close to you. Furthermore, the conflicts that are found in your household are mere reflections of the conflicts that you find within yourself. Undertaking those conflicts on the outer level means undertaking them on the inner level as well. No purification is possible, and therefore, no spiritual growth is possible without this particular undertaking. Here the entire subject of hatred of parents is brought up. It is explained in greater detail in the commentary on Number Sixty.

Notice what is missing from the corresponding passages in the Bible, Matthew 10:34-36: "Do not think that I have come to bring peace on Earth; I have not come to bring peace, but a sword. For I have come to set a man against his father, and a daughter against her mother, and a daughter-in-law against her mother-in-law; and a man's foes will be those of his own household."

All of *"they will be lifted up, being solitaries"* has been totally omitted from the accepted Bible text. When Christianity became a conventional and accepted religion, the concept of being lifted up by entering into conflict with one's relatives became a very dangerous one. Indeed, what if members of the Catholic "Mother" Church underwent a massive questioning of their faith, of the Pope's infallibility, of the whole hierarchical church system, not to mention all of the obvious outrages and contradictions to be found throughout the entire organization? So, conveniently, *"and they will be lifted up, being solitaries"* disappeared from all texts.

# NUMBER EIGHTEEN

Jesus says: *"I will give you what eye has never seen, and what ear has never heard, and what hand has never touched, and what has never entered into the heart of man."*

"*I will give you,*" he says, that which is original, clean, never expressed in this particular way. And indeed, he did when he said, for instance, that instead of an eye for an eye, you should turn the other cheek. He taught concepts and ways of life that had never been conceived of, although, in another sense, they were already known in other places.

Jesus' teachings about resisting not evil can be compared to the Buddha's Four Noble Truths. He brought these teachings to the Jewish world, which was his world, and contrasted them to the existing Old Testament teachings. In that sense, he was a revolutionary, bringing in teachings that appear to be, and sometimes were, contrary to the ones that heretofore had been taught and followed.

What Jesus was in essence doing, was to correct the ways in which Spiritual Law had been violated through the literal following of, as an example, the Ten Commandments. Great repetition will change the interpretation of words and expressions. They become devoid of power and crystallized when repeated too often. He was expressing in new words the same old teaching. However, since the old words had become devoid of meaning the new words appear to contradict the old teachings.

The present dispensation, the New Age dispensation, is doing this again, bringing ways of life, concepts, a new view of the universe, that heretofore have never existed, that are totally original. The eye, the ear, the heart have never seen or comprehended such a broad understanding of the universe or had available such excellent tools for healing as now.

This saying also points to the necessity to continuously look for what the eye has never seen, the ear has never heard, etc.—the new, that which is in continuous change, in continuous flux. Be continuously in awe, keep your Instinct of Enquiry alive, and you will be alive and you will be at-one with God.

# NUMBER NINETEEN

*The disciples say to Jesus: "Tell us what our end will be." Jesus says: "Have you then deciphered the beginning, that you ask about the end? For where the beginning is, there shall be the end. Blessed is the man who reaches the beginning; he will know the end, and will not taste death!"*

This demonstrates that psychoanalysis existed two thousand years ago. Indeed, the Christ, in response to His disciples asking Him to predict the future or the end, urges them to go to the beginning. If you go to the beginning of your life you will find there the key to your life and, therefore, the key to the end. At the point you make the connection between the beginning and the end, there will be no end, you will be immortal, you will have found immortality. The answer to all your problems lies in the discovery of early childhood experiences in which the soul was powerfully imprinted by misconceptions, by ways of life that are against Spiritual Law. It is by understanding and reliving and dissolving these misconceptions that we find solutions to all our problems and that we find immortality.

Psychology, the study of the soul, merely borrowed from this spiritual practice. The Path was a spiritual practice long before it was approved of or sanctioned by any state, by Caesar. Therefore, psychology does not make sense unless it is connected to spirituality. The study of the soul must have for a goal the immortality of the soul. It must be understood in the context of spirituality, otherwise, it will die a death of despair, as did Freud. See also Number Four of this commentary.

It is no use trying to find out what will happen in the future if you do not understand your past. This also points to the fallacy of predictions. It is very unfortunate that astrologers, tarot card readers and so forth are so closely identified with the New Age. A prediction can have a nefarious effect on an individual, as it becomes a self-fulfilling prophesy. If somebody tells you that on a particular date something wonderful is going to happen to you there are two possibilities:

1) It actually happens; this is the worst possibility since you are now addicted to having predictions made for you. You have lost your connection with the Law of Cause and Effect; you have lost your faith in creating your own reality. The astrologer or the tarot reader has created the reality for you.

2) It does not happen. Then you are disappointed. This opens the door to seeing the universe as chaotic, to losing faith.

Predictions are disastrous. Only when the causal connections between past and present are established can the future be understood as a possibility, as a potential, as a probability, **not** as a certainty. The future can change and does change.

# NUMBER TWENTY

*Jesus says: "Blessed is the man who existed before he came into being!"*

Meaning, blessed is he who is aware of essence before its manifestation. When we come into being, i.e., when we are born, we are already precipitated. The necessary loss of memory of the past is also a function of our distortions as we penetrate the three-dimensional world. Gradually, we recover the memory of essence, of that which we were before coming into being. This is the process of enlightenment. This saying is connected to the previous one in which the Christ urges us to dig into our past and to make causal connections between past and present. Making causal connections between essence and manifestation is the same.

Where did you come from? What existed before this life? Do you remember anything before your birth? Have you tried to? Sometimes in childhood, before puberty, there are a lot of karmic memories. Do you remember any, do you have any? If you do, see if you can make the connection between those and the circumstances of your present life. The goal of all of this, of course, must be and always is the pursuit of happiness.

Caution: I am not here in any way encouraging the reliance on past life knowledge in order to explain away and rationalize present events. Do not escape into past lives. The exercise here is to try to remember or judiciously to be told by a teacher who cares for you enough to impart information to you that can be used immediately.

You do not need information coming from any other life but this one. You have recreated in your present soul substance everything that you need to understand anything and everything about yourself. By resolving what has happened in this life, you can resolve what has happened in past lives without ever being aware of the events of those lives. For example, if somebody had a problem of greed in a past life, he will create conditions in this life that will bring back the greed. By working on those conditions and by working on the manifestations of the greed in this life he will also resolve the karma that he carries from the greediness of all the past lives.

# NUMBER TWENTY-ONE

*"If you become my disciples and if you hear my words, these stones will serve you."*

Frankly, I do not quite know what the Christ means here. Is He referring to healing through stones? Or perhaps He is indicating that the most common things you can find in life will serve you as Christ's disciple.

With the help of my friends, here is more meaning to this one:

- The words of Christ are like stones with which you can build. They are meaningful beliefs which can guide you. Also, He referred to Peter as the stone on which He would build His church.
- If you become My disciples and hear My words, everything in life, including these mere stones, will have meaning and be of help.

# NUMBER TWENTY-TWO

*"For you have there, in Paradise, five trees which change not winter nor summer, whose leaves do not fall: whoever knows them will not taste death!"*

Here the Christ is referring to fundamental truths which remain the same, do not change with seasons, do not get old. If you know them you will have eternal life. He does not tell us what the five trees are, these five truths. We know of the Four Noble Truths of Buddha. He is obviously not talking about the Ten Commandments.

# NUMBER TWENTY-THREE

*The disciples say to Jesus: "Tell us what the Kingdom of heaven is like!" He says to them: "It is like a grain of mustard: it is smaller than all the [other] seeds, but when it falls on ploughed land it produces a big stalk and becomes a shelter for the birds of heaven!"*

The Christ is trying to explain to primitive mankind the fact that the Kingdom of Heaven has absolutely no relationship to criteria of big and small, tall and large, etc. The best way he can find to explain this is to compare it to a mustard seed which *"is smaller than all other seeds,"* in other words, infinitely small, but which carries potential, the potential of life and the potential of protection if it falls on ploughed land. Ploughed land is our soul, our fertile soul. We plough our soul when we under go the processes of purification as found on this Path. The ploughing of the soul makes it receptive to being impregnated by the seed of the Kingdom of Heaven which then produces in our three-dimensional reality a big stalk, i.e., we become someone who provides protection. You can be a teacher, a healer, a giver of knowledge for those who do not know their way and who have no sense of direction. The big stalk becomes a point of reference, a landmark where we find rest and shelter, a place of safety.

# NUMBER TWENTY-FOUR

*Mary says to Jesus: "Who are your disciples like?" He says to her: "They are like little children who have made their way into a field that does not belong to them. When the owners of the field come, they will say: 'Get out of our field!' They [then] will give up the field to these [people] and let them have their field back again."*

In this description of His disciples, the Christ says a lot.

1. *"They are like little children."* One can imagine the despair and the discouragement that the Christ must have felt teaching these incredibly evolved concepts to poorly educated and spiritually limited people. At the same time, seeing them for the little children they were must have helped Him persevere. We should do the same with all of those we are trying to teach, have patience and perseverance. We should do likewise with our lower self which is very much like Christ's disciples, a little child with whom you have patience and perseverance, with whom you use symbolism, parables, who you have to motivate using carrot and stick, whose path you have to illuminate and whose thoughts, feelings, and actions you have to mind.

2. *"...who have made their way into a field that does not belong to them."* This is obviously the Kingdom of Heaven, the field of knowledge that the Christ is bringing, the new dispensation. The children go to a field that they have not been to before, that does not belong to them. They make that field their own. This describes the arrogant process of claiming the concepts as their own. To begin with, the ideas do not belong to those to whom the concepts are imparted;

they are divine. Then, the children try to make them their own by putting these concepts into words, by distorting them, by claiming that they are the sole dispensers of the new religion and therefore,

3. *"When the owners of the field come, they will say: 'Get out of our field!'"* When the divine guidance that has dispensed the new teachings comes back and tries to tell them, Look, this is not your field, the children will not recognize the rightful owners and will chase them away. This is when those religions arrogantly claim to be close to God, or God Himself. When God or new teachings attempt to come in and talk to them and tell them that they have distorted the original dispensation, they do not listen and they chase the owners away.

Note: In case we interpret this to mean that the owners claim back their field, the same explanation holds. Eventually the owners of the field end up occupying that field again, i.e., giving yet another new dispensation to the children. And these children who distorted the original dispensation will have to give up their position as the accepted conventional religion and make room for the new.

# NUMBER TWENTY-FIVE

*"That is why I tell you this: If the master of the house knows that the thief is coming, he will watch before he comes and will not allow him to force an entry into his royal house to carry off its furniture. You, then, be on the watch against the world. Gird your loins with great energy, so that the brigands do not find any way of reaching you; for they will find any place you fail to watch."*

This refers to the necessity of protecting new dispensations. We here at The Church of the Path® have learned how threatening those new teachings can be. Since they are new teachings, they have spared no one, none of the existing institutions are exempted. They are all attacked in their negativity and in their lower self. The massive defensive counterattack that comes from this is enormous.

The forces of darkness are much more interested in attacking people who are developed than in attacking those who are not. They are not interested in destroying people who are not evolved. The more an individual becomes an agent of light the more the dark forces will focus on that person, trying to neutralize him or to destroy him.

And you have to be vigilant about every place within yourself, *"for they will find any place you fail to watch."* This refers to the oft-mentioned process of looking at all of your lower self, of not leaving one stone unturned. Any space in your life, however small, that contains negativity is a target for infiltration of evil. This becomes particularly and painfully true the more you grow spiritually. The more evolved you become the less you can afford to have the slightest bit of lower self in your system. If you let it, it will magnify exponentially, proving this saying: that the thief will *"find any place you fail to watch."*

Here again is a picture of a vigorous Christ, a Christ who fights, who protects Himself, protects others, urges you to protect yourself, to even resort to violence if you have to in order to protect yourself. This is not at all the namby-pamby victimized Christ as represented by conventional religion.

# NUMBER TWENTY-SIX

*"Let there be among you [such] a prudent man: when the fruit arrived, quickly, sickle in hand, he went and harvested it. He who has ears to hear, let him hear!"*

Do not waste time. Take advantage of every opportunity that comes to you. If you do not, the opportunities will turn negative, first challenging you, then propelling you into crisis.

Christ is also teaching us about timeliness. When the fruit arrives, i.e., on the very day it ripens, that is when it has to be cut and eaten, assimilated. The moment of opportunity has to be seized. In sports, this is very well known as the "sweet spot," when the tennis racket and the ball meet at the ideal time and point. Then effortlessly the ball is struck with a maximum of precision and speed. It is also true of all other actions, thoughts, feelings, words. Let yourself react in a timely fashion. Let yourself speak the right words at the right time. Understand and become aware of the healthy balance that exists in tension and live in the middle of it. This constitutes love.

Reflecting further on this, I find more. I think He is telling His disciples that the opportunity is at hand. The opportunity is, of course, His presence. He is the fruit, the fruit is ripe; the Word is given. So He tells them to recognize it, to take full advantage of it, to use it as much as they can. Implicit in this is the caution not to take it for granted because it is not going to be here always—it comes rhythmically and seasonally.

It reminds me of how one takes for granted a teacher

and learns the hard way after their death. We find out how much we miss that which we thought would always be there—their presence and the availability of guidance on the outer level. In the last analysis, it is a blessing, but things would be been far easier if one made full use of their presence. I am sure Christ's disciples felt the same at the time of His death.

# NUMBER TWENTY-SEVEN

*Jesus saw some children who were taking the breast: he said to his disciples: "These little ones who suck are like those who enter the Kingdom." They said to him: "If we are little, shall we enter the Kingdom?" Jesus says to them: "When you make the two [become] one, and when you make the inside like the outside and the outside like the inside, and the upper like the lower! And if you make the male and the female one, so that the male is no longer male and the female no longer female, and when you put eyes in the place of an eye, and a hand in the place of a hand, and a foot in the place of a foot, and an image in the place of an image, then you will enter [the Kingdom!"]*

The little ones who suck are like those who enter the Kingdom. It takes childlike simplicity to enter. You cannot penetrate the Kingdom with your baggage—whether this baggage be material, emotional, or mental. You must let go of all of the misconceptions that you hold onto and advance naked into the Kingdom, naked as the little ones are, innocent.

To which the disciples respond, "*if we are little, shall we enter the Kingdom?*," exhibiting that they are children in the worst possible way. "O, Master, what do I have to do to enter the Kingdom, what card do I play, what mask do I put on, do I make myself little, do I make myself innocent, do I pretend to be cute?" This demonstrates that they are going about it the wrong way, that they believe that by pretending to be something they are not, by making themselves little, by acting innocent they can enter the Kingdom. Not so! It resembles conventional religion which has cut off the beauty of sexuality through abstinence, thus making "believers" into preadolescent children; Christianity has lost itself in syrupy and sickly sweet religious practices, worshipping victimization, weakness and poverty, and has defined its founder as an impotent and ineffectual "Man of Sorrows" saviour who grants vicarious redemption to His bovine flock. All of this, being artificially and superficially little, has absolutely no resemblance to spirituality. It will not get anybody anywhere near the kingdom of God.

By contrast, here is how to do it:

1) "Make the two become one," meaning transcend duality, work on the contradictory parts of yourself as we do on the Path. We identify those as the mother-father split (see Glossary).

2) "Make the inside like the outside and the outside like the inside," meaning establish causal connections between that which is inside of you and that which is outside of you. What is inside of you creates that which is outside of you; as long as you believe that there is a difference between the two you are deluding yourself, you are living a lie. Untruths themselves are a manifestation of the disconnection between the outside and the inside. The author of a lie believes that what he says on the outside can be different from what he thinks and feels on the inside. All of these disconnections have to be unified, brought together.

3) Make "the upper like the lower." Here the Christ is talking about the higher duality, i.e., good versus evil. When the lower duality is worked out—the inside and the outside, then the upper and the lower can become unified. This is the crucifixion of the ego as we understand it.

4) "Make the male and the female one, so that the male

is no longer male and the female is no longer female," i.e., explore the other side of yourself. If you are a man, you must explore the female existing inside yourself; if you are a woman, you must explore the male inside of yourself. By doing so you bring the two sides together. This is the meaning of sexuality, the meaning of relationship and union with another being—union of male and female within one's self. Only when a person is engaged in intimate union with another being on the outer level, **and** intimate union on the inner level with the other side of his/her own being is (s)he on the way to becoming at-one with the Universal Life Force and, therefore, able to enter the Kingdom. Here is also proof positive of the Christ's teaching of the sanctity of sexuality and equality of the sexes. Let there be no other interpretation of this in spite of saying Number One Hundred Eighteen in which the Christ seems to condone Simon Peter's saying that women are not worthy of life. It is not true; the Christ always respected women as being equal to men and urged them to enter the Kingdom on the same level as males.

5) "Put eyes in the place of an eye, and a hand in the place of a hand, and a foot in the place of a foot." The existence of two eyes, two hands, and two feet is an out-picturing of our duality. The unification of all of these brings unity of sight, one universal vision, one action, one creativity, and one concept of God and of the kingdom. When this is achieved, when total unity is accomplished then you can enter the kingdom of God.

This is further clarified by "an image in the place of an image." When two images are superimposed exactly on top of one another they merge. When the two eyes become the same they will merge into one; each eye needs to meet the other by seeing in the other its own likeness, as in two lovers recognizing themselves in the other when they come together. When unified in its purpose, each hand will go with the other towards a single end.

# NUMBER TWENTY-EIGHT

*Jesus says: "I will choose you, one from a thousand and two from ten thousand, and those [whom I have chosen] will be lifted up, being one!"*

This saying confirms the scarcity of people who are ready to be Christ's followers. Those who are ready to be lifted up are few and far between. In fact, the more people you consider, the less you will find who are ready for the Kingdom, as demonstrated by the exponential increase in ratio—one from one thousand and two from ten thousand.

Here at The Church of the Path®, we experience this very dramatically. Many people come to us. They take a workshop. They sporadically come to services. They attend an occasional lecture. Then they disappear, not to be seen again.

Only one out of a great many of them sees the value of this difficult Path. Once this understanding is reached, the person's commitment is great; nothing else satisfies him but the stark naked pursuit of happiness the way it is understood by the true disciples of the Christ, i.e., by people who are on the Path.

Those who are most ready for the word are attracted to the light; you find one in a thousand around the Christ, around the light. In order to find a crowd of ten thousand you have to get farther away from the Christ. Therefore, you find a lot fewer candidates. The thousand people closest to Christ are many times more enlightened than the next nine thousand people who are one tier removed from that first thousand. Therefore, out of the first thousand there might be one, but out of the next nine thousand there might be only one more. This, therefore, is "one from a thousand and two from ten thousand."

What about this business of choice? Is the Christ arbitrarily "choosing" those who will be lifted up? How is the choice made? The choice is made by tests.

Some pass the initial test, will enter into the work and at some point or other will fail. They are then asked to leave, they are not chosen; they are called, but they are not chosen.

In order to continue in this pursuit of spirituality and search for the center, one has to continuously undergo change. This change requires a divestiture of one layer after another. Just like an onion, a person has to shed all of his layers until he is left with the core—then he has made it to the Kingdom. If he refuses to shed a layer when it is ready to be shed, he is rejected and he is no longer chosen. Those who are chosen are those who are continuously willing to shed any and all layers that keep them from the light.

For example, very dear friends of ours, who were founders of this church, underwent great transformational progress, taking them from a state of virtual seclusion to a position of comfort, self-acceptance, societal status and professional success. Once they acquired a house they changed. The ownership of this house arrested their progress, as if reaching that level was for them the final accomplishment.

Unconsciously, they may have both had this as an ultimate end, perhaps even a goal that they never thought they would attain; reaching it made all other goals abhorrent, including the spiritual objective of participation in a community effort. For the sake of their newly found position that they did not want to give up, they betrayed their commitments and their leadership in our community. This was the onion layer on which they became stuck. Who knows whether they will get unstuck in this lifetime or in the next few lifetimes; who knows when the opportunity will return to once again accelerate their path in the same manner as in the past seven years.

They are not the only examples. Another very committed person in our group chose to regress, to capitulate to his mother and betray his responsibilities to the church and to his wife. And another person decided that keeping her marriage intact was more important than keeping her soul intact. She sold her soul and she sold her position on the Path for the sake of keeping her marriage. Others have taken a different attitude. They chose to break their marriage but remain on the Path, continuing to shed more layers, and after a while they have found each other again, but this time on a different and much higher level.

Generally speaking, we find that people stop shedding layers when they reach what they regard to be their "goal," whether that goal is understood on the conscious level or whether it is unconscious. It is as if the positive results themselves constitute an impediment to the continuation of a person's spiritual progress. The outer level progress becomes the layer of the onion on which the individual holds for dear life.

Unfortunately, all of these people know very well that their departure is a betrayal of their soul. They all feel guilty about it but they are too ashamed to admit the guilt. Instead, they build cases against the Path, as Judas built a case against the Christ, as Saul of Tarsus built a case against the Christians before he converted and became Paul.

You are "chosen" as long as you continue on your path at whatever the cost. The minute you stop you are no longer chosen. You stop because you do not want to take an opportunity for growth. Then you encounter a challenge. When you do not meet the challenge, a crisis takes you over and you are no longer chosen. When you drop out, real damage is done on the spiritual level, even though on the material level consequences are not felt—not right away anyway. However, I guarantee that there are severe consequences in the future *on the outer level*.

# NUMBER TWENTY-NINE

*His disciples say to him: "Instruct us about the place where thou art, for we must know about it!" He says to them: "He who has ears, let him hear! If a light exists inside a luminous one, then it gives light to the whole world; but if it does not give light, [it means that it is] a darkness."*

Here is another attempt by the disciples to get quick answers from the Christ. They want to know how to arrive at the place of light in which He is to be found. Again, He says to them to listen with the inner ear; look for the light within yourself, the light emitted by your Higher Self.

Our task on the Path is to find this light, to nurture it and to cultivate it. When that light is found, it is not only our personal life that is being illuminated but the entire world. Each person has for a task to illuminate the entire world in a specific fashion. When all created beings are again "luminous," the Plan of Salvation will have been consummated.

There are those who do not emit light. They are still in darkness. The Christ is urging His disciples to develop the ability to tell where the light is and where the darkness is in different people by opening the inner ear. There is an implied admonishing here. He warns of false teachers, of people who are actually in darkness but who pretend that they are emitting light. He also says that the only way to make that differentiation is through the inner ear which, therefore, we must cultivate.

# NUMBER THIRTY

*Jesus says: "Love thy brother like thy soul; watch over him like the apple of thine eye."*

In order to understand this saying, we must remember that the soul is not all positive, it contains elements of negativity which at some point are released into the individual's personality so they can be resolved. Loving your brother like your soul, therefore, means accepting his imperfections, accepting the good and accepting the bad in him the way you accept the good and the bad in your own soul. Watching over your brother like the apple of your eye does not mean only selfless giving, it also means sensitivity to your brother's soul as if it were yours. Both your soul and your brother's have to be accepted, nurtured, protected and used. They also have to be kept clean and free of obstructions so as to allow continuous vision and apprehension of reality.

# NUMBER THIRTY-ONE

*Jesus says: "The straw that is in thy brother's eye, thou seest; but the beam that is in thine own eye, thou seest not! When thou hast cast out the beam that is in thine own eye, then thou wilt see to cast out the straw from thy brother's eye."*

This saying very much pertains to the code of conduct that we hold on the Path:

1. Before accusing somebody else of a fault, look at yourself and see if you actually have this same defect within yourself. It goes further: if you find yourself heavily blaming somebody else then you can be certain that you are blind to the same issue within yourself. If you did not have this particular fault you would not mind it so much in others. There are other types of defects in people that you do not mind that much. This is a confirmation that you yourself must have it on some level. Look for it and find it before you accuse somebody else of having it.

2. If you hear somebody maligning a third party, it is your duty to go to the person who has been maligned with the person who has done the maligning and clarify the entire matter. It is very damaging to everyone concerned to talk ill of people behind their backs.

3. Only after you have purified yourself will you be able to see clearly what is in others and to respond healthily to them. As long as you harbor negativity, your perception and response to others will be warped by the beam that is in your own eye.

# NUMBER THIRTY-TWO

*"If you do not fast from the world, you will not find the Kingdom. If you do not make the Sabbath the [true] Sabbath, you will not see the Father."*

What is the real meaning of fasting from the world? If you will reread the case histories that we mentioned in the commentary of Number Twenty-Eight you will understand what is meant here. Fasting from the world means being willing to give up that which is of the world. You enter the Kingdom naked and without baggage; you take with you absolutely nothing that you have gained from the three-dimensional world except the lessons you have learned.

Making the Sabbath the true Sabbath is also related to this. Indeed, during the Sabbath, if it is respected correctly, Jewish tradition requires that you do absolutely nothing. For example: lighting a fire on the Sabbath is forbidden, so is cooking, pulling your ox out of the ditch, etc. The rigor here, of course, is an exaggeration. However, the kernel of truth to be found in it is the absolute relinquishing of worldly concerns that has to occur at least once a week in order to find God through prayer. It is this same relinquishing that is referred to in the first part of this saying in Christ's requirement to fast from the world.

In our faith, we extend this. We recommend that a Sabbath be respected daily. Every day, carve out of your schedule time in which you do nothing, when you merely observe your thoughts and then gradually enter into meditation. This creative emptiness is absolutely necessary to attract the Universal Life Force—God. You have to fast—create an emptiness, a vacuum—in order to be filled by the Universal Life Force.

Furthermore, finding the Kingdom is seeing the Father—and vice versa. One cannot exist without the other. Here is the bringing together of immanence and transcendence—immanence in finding the Kingdom and transcendence in seeing God the Father.

# NUMBER THIRTY-THREE

*Jesus says: "I stood in the midst of the world, and in the flesh I manifested myself to them. I found them all drunk; I found none athirst among them. And my soul was afflicted for the children of men. Because they are blind in their heart and do not see, because they have come into the world empty, [that is why] they seek still to go out from the world empty. But let someone come who will correct them! Then, when they have slept off their wine, they will repent."*

Compare this to Number Six in which the Christ minimizes physical fasting (not indulging in food or drink) and emphasizes ethical behaviour. This confirms that the fast He is referring to has to do with the relinquishing of those attachments which in our eyes are superior to God Himself—the house, the job, the diploma, the status.... We prefer to give more value to these than to ethical behaviour or commitment.

Compare it also to Number Fifteen, "when you fast you will beget sin for yourselves, when you pray you will be condemned, when you give alms you will do evil to your souls." The value of a fast depends on why you fast, not how you fast. In my youth as a Jew in Alexandria, Egypt where there was a large Jewish community, everybody dressed up to a T on the day of fasting, Yom Kippur, the Day of Atonement. Everybody was fasting but everybody was also wearing their most sumptuous outfits. They were showing off. It was more a social occasion than anything else. It was an opportunity to act out the mass glamour of self-importance, the part of us that screams to high heaven

"Me! Me! Me! Pay attention to me!" This type of fasting is not only worthless, it is also regressive, destructive, and damaging.

Standing "in the midst of the world," Christ speaks, of course, of His incarnation and of His task. As a Master He can materialize and dematerialize at will; He can choose to incarnate and discarnate as well. Here it is the Christ who is actually talking, not Jesus. Jesus, the personality, was the owner of the body and had to go through the process of growing up and had to learn that the Christ had chosen Him as a channel. It is the Christ who stands in the midst of the world and who manifests in the flesh at will.

"I found them all drunk; I found none athirst among them": they are not thirsty because they are drunk, drunk with half measures, with compromises, with quick fixes, with approval seeking. Drunk as in numb, numb to their real needs, numb to their primary feelings. If they were aware of their real needs and their primary feelings, they would be thirsty and they would be conscious, awake, aware, alive. If, in the satisfaction of our needs, we compromise in order to quench our thirst quickly, we never get satisfied. The nature of the compromise itself brings only partial satisfaction. As we say in our prayers, "total longing brings total fulfillment;" partial longing brings partial fulfillment. Partial fulfillment brings addictive behaviour, the behaviour of someone who is never satisfied.

All addictions come from this same compromising place. Sometimes one finds layers upon layers of compromises leading to layers upon layers of addictions. For instance, if as a child you felt that you were not entirely loved, you started settling for approval. The approval did not quite satisfy you so you demanded it; you made yourself into what they wanted you to be to get more approval. However, once you became what they wanted you to be, still you were not satisfied and still you did not get what **you** wanted. So you started drinking, which is another layer of compromise. You believed that at least in the bottle you would find the abandonment or the satisfaction missing in the seeking of approval or the conforming. The bottle is then invested with the job of totally satisfying your longing for the Universal Life Force, which is impossible.

If you stop drinking, you will remain afraid of starting again. That is because you have not gone deep enough to look for the causes of that alcoholism. You do not have enough faith in yourself to realize that the total, blissful abandonment that you thought you were going to get through the bottle is actually a state that is your birthright and can only be obtained through not compromising, through the total and unconditional pursuit of happiness under absolutely ethical behaviour. Believing that this state of grace exists will make you thirsty again, will make you long again, will put you in touch again with your instinctual needs. **Then** you will be thirsty for the Christ and what He has to say.

"And my soul was afflicted for the children of men." His affliction is our affliction. We find ourselves sometimes at a loss to understand why so few are open to the teachings of this Path. Many of us spend a lot of time and effort trying to introduce these lessons to those who we believe are ready for it, only to meet with disappointment.

Our despair is His despair. And since behind every despair there is a demand, His despair was also His demand. As do we on some level, He demands that more people be ready to receive these teachings. So did Martin Luther demand that more people listen to him, so did Copernicus and Galileo, etc. In expressing this despair, both Christ and Jesus demonstrate Their humanity. They are not perfect.

Only God does not have demands and does not have despair. It is extremely important to understand this, that the great demonstration of Christ on Earth is imperfection. His cry on the cross, "Why has thou forsaken me," demonstrates His imperfection. If He feels forsaken by God, it means that He is imperfect.

One cannot be perfect and be forsaken by God; if one has achieved perfection, one is not forsaken. We can be in contact with God to the degree that we are able to understand our imperfection and disengage from it. This then immediately puts us in contact with perfection here and now.

Perfection is life, it is available here and now if the imperfections are realized and seen. Since they are finite they can be identified and not identified with. The infinite must be identified with once the finite is identified.

The next sentence explains the difficulty of growing. If somebody is "blind in his heart," he does not feel. Once again, we have a numb and drunken state described here. If you do not see, you cannot advance, since you must see in order to progress. The Law of Visualization says this very clearly, nothing is ever achieved unless it is visualized, be it positive or negative.

In order to visualize, one has to desire and long. The desire itself creates the visualization, is the visualization. The existence of the desire proves that a better state exists than the one that is experienced here and now—only by experiencing my dissatisfaction do I know that there exists a better state than the one I am in right now. Therefore, dissatisfaction carries in it the promise of satisfaction; the experience of pain guarantees pleasure; visualization assures materialization.

The rest of the sentence describes this drunkenness, this blindness in the heart, as an emptiness. If you remain empty, you have nothing to give, that is all you know. This is otherwise known as poverty consciousness. If you do not open your mind to the existence of riches, you will always remain poor. If all you have within yourself is emptiness, then you will always remain empty and want to remain empty, considering fullness as dangerous, as an unknown.

In our day and time, the majority of humanity is empty, being born empty and dying empty. Surely we see this in the Third World which constitutes the overwhelming majority of humanity. This was certainly true two thousand years ago when this gospel was written.

How do you get off the wheel? One comes into the world empty and one leaves the world empty. Where and how does one get off that circle? You stay in that circle for a vast period of time. If you consider that your career with humanity consists of 500 to 800 incarnations and only in the last ten or twenty incarnations are you in the light, and you enter the Path certainly in the last ten or less incarnations, you begin to realize that you have spent most of your lifetimes round and round the wheel of karma. You get off when you open your consciousness to a better state.

If you look at the process of saying, "there must be a better state than this," you realize it comes from a place of pain which says, "the state in which I am right now is not comfortable." As long as you do not say this to yourself, you do not experience that the state you are in right now is unsatisfactory. Only when you start saying that it is unsatisfactory do you start feeling the pain of the dissatisfaction, and you start remembering that there is a better state. And only **then** do you start doing something about freeing yourself from that wheel. This is done very very gradually.

One of the great values of studying history is to see this process occurring for humanity. Then you realize it is not as a wheel but as a spiral—it acquires one additional dimension. And you see that getting off the wheel is a gradual process and an accelerating one. What do you get when you project a spiral on a two dimensional plane? You get a sine curve. That, too, is a good out-picturing of how the Path works, progress is an ever accelerating sine curve.

There are worlds that are less developed than the human world, where cause is so disconnected from effect that it seems impossible for those who are caught in it to get out. When somebody on our plane of existence acts as if the Law of Cause and Effect does not exist, that is exactly what he creates for himself. He is then relegated to a world in which it does not exist or exists so remotely that it is not apparent. The disconnection of cause from effect brings only pain, the pain of injustice and victimization for "acts of God" and life events that seemingly happen for no reason. This is hell.

The minute you remove the Law of Cause and Effect you fall into one of two possibilities:

1. A victimizer in which you ruthlessly take advantage, rape, pillage and plunder for your own selfishness without ever wanting to feel guilt or any of the consequences that come from it.

2. A victim who always blames the world for his own problems. He allows himself to be raped, pillaged and

plundered, expecting somebody else to come to his defense and rescue.

People alternate between the first and second and then back to the first. When you do one, you open the possibility of becoming the other at the point when you burn out.

Germany the victimizer became Germany the victimized at the end of World War II. Germans reincarnate into Jews and Jews into Germans. This explains the militaristic and bellicose nature of the state of Israel which reminds us so much of Hitleric Germany. The Germans, having lived so royally during the years of World War II found themselves in utter famine and poverty at the end of it. Those who escaped with treasures and millions and who died seemingly impunitively met the Being of Light. At that point, they experienced in one flash all of the pain that they had inflicted on every single human being on Earth. They experienced what it feels like to be robbed to the exact measure that they robbed others. This is the Law of Cause and Effect in action. The magnitude of the outrage distances a person from the Law of Cause and Effect. It seems as if they will never be able to repay for all of the misery they have created. That is what it is like to live outside the Law of Cause and Effect. It is the worst nightmare imaginable in human existence. It is the experience of the pain of injustice perpetuated.

"But let someone come who will correct them." He is here, of course, describing His own task, as well as the task of all of those who herald new teachings, new discoveries. They are there to correct the course of events of humanity. This, of course, makes this Path a very difficult one. We are not here to be good old blokes who conform to what is going on. We are here to teach, we are here to reverse currents, we are here to correct, we are here to clean up Aegean stables[1]. The task is not an easy one. Once you "have slept off your wine," you repent.

"Let someone come who will correct them" is also an instruction to us to be teachers in that same way. It is an invitation.

---

[1] A Labor of Hercules.

# NUMBER THIRTY-FOUR

*Jesus says: "If the flesh was produced for the sake of the spirit, it is a miracle. But if the spirit [was produced] for the sake of the body, it is a miracle of a miracle." But for myself (?), I marvel at that because the [...of] this (?) great wealth has dwelt in this poverty.*

The fact that the flesh was produced for the sake of the spirit is well known and oft-mentioned. Indeed, we know that flesh must be an instrument of the spirit. However, was the flesh produced for the sake of the spirit or was the flesh produced because the spirit faltered? If the flesh is a deceleration of spirit, it certainly was not produced **for** the spirit, but in spite of it. We can, of course, lose ourselves in the philosophical considerations that result from this type of thinking—not my reason for writing this commentary.

The purpose of this saying is evident when we consider the second sentence in contrast to the first, i.e., the spirit at the service of the body being an even greater miracle than the body at the service of the spirit. I believe the Christ is contrasting our search for God, the process of putting our flesh in the service of spirit, in contradistinction to God's spirits' service to us. During His lifetime, the Christ made a big point of demonstrating that He was a servant of humanity—washing His disciples' feet, etc. What about the help we get every single day of our lives from unseen spirit guides, inner guidance? It is unimaginable in its scope. The miracle is the existence of this infinite guidance that is available to us. This help is totally anonymous. Spirits of God usually do not identify themselves. If they do, it is kept to a minimum so the process of helping us remains as discrete as possible. Compared to the miracle of our search for God, God's help to us is a much greater miracle.

In the last sentence, the Christ marvels at the great wealth of the spirit dwelling in the poverty of the flesh. It is the infinite dwelling in the finite. And that indeed is marvelous! This is why I believe that the missing word in the text should be "vastness" or "infinity;" the sentence reading: "But for myself, I marvel at that because the vastness of this great wealth has dwelt in this poverty."

Reflecting further on the meaning of this as far as our New Age is concerned, this saying yields even more connections. Indeed, what differentiates the New Age from all the other ages is the fact that for the first time in the history of humanity spirit penetrates matter in order to purify it. Heretofore, the individual had to disengage, disconnect from matter in order to reach the spirit. It has been a dualistic process. It is now becoming much more of a unitive process in that the spirit, while penetrating matter, accelerates it, purifies it and unifies with it. The in-dwelling spirit contained in the flesh is becoming more and more marvelous in our New Age.

# NUMBER THIRTY-FIVE

*Jesus says: "There where there are three gods, they are gods. Where there are two, or [else] one, I am with him!"*

The three gods referred to here are obviously the three Rays of Aspect[2]. In the times and places where the three of Rays of Aspect are present and are harmonious, they are at-one with God, they are gods.

Here the Christ recognizes that he who has completed the harmonious blending of the three Rays of Aspect within himself has become God. The blending of the three Rays of Aspect which I am describing here does not necessarily apply to one individual. It can apply to a civilization, or it can apply to a specific area in an individual's life, or it can apply to one act as in, for instance, a perfectly executed forehand topspin in tennis, which is divine. This applies to anything anywhere in microcosm and in macrocosm.

However, when the blending is incomplete, i.e., when only one or two aspects are present, then the Christ Himself offers His presence to complete the triad. By looking for Him we actually are looking for the missing aspect(s). Conversely, by looking for anything that is lacking within ourselves and replacing it, we find Him, we find the Christ, we find at-onement with God.

Here again, we find the fundamental theme of the Path, which is the focusing on that which is lacking within one's self and the subsequent work to make the needed

---

[2] Energies of Will, Love, and Active Intelligence (Rays I, II, and III). See commentary Number Four for a discussion of the Rays and Glossary.

corrections and mend the hurts. Any discipline, or religion, or path, or philosophy that does not include this activity of self-betterment, self-purification and self-completion is worthless.

# NUMBER THIRTY-SIX

*Jesus says: "A prophet is not accepted in his [own] city, and a doctor does not heal those who know him."*

The reason a prophet is not accepted in his own city is because the people who have known him all his life will not accept him as a teacher. The teacher emerges later in life, usually at age twenty eight or after.

No one would accept that the carpenter they knew as a child had suddenly become a great prophet and teacher. Christianity was not accepted by the Jews, even though it was born in the midst of Judaism at the eastern end of the Mediterranean. However, it became the religion of the West which resides at the opposite end of the Mediterranean.

In the city of Medina, nobody accepted Mohammed. They threw him out. He fled to Mecca with his wife and his best friend, and it is only in Mecca that he started a new religion.

The Christ then relates this to the doctor and his inability to heal those who know him. Personal involvement interferes with the process of healing. In order for the process of healing to be effective, it has to be practiced with healthy detachment.

For example, if you were a surgeon, could you operate on your child's heart or brain? Even if you could, would you do it?

Let's carry this point further to the transferential situation that exists between counselor and counseled or between healer and healee. Let us also expand "knowing" to its biblical sense. What we get then is that if there is emotional or sexual involvement between counselor and counseled, healer and healee, doctor and patient, then healing cannot proceed in a healthy manner.

The teacher, the doctor, the helper, the counselor cannot allow himself to be involved on a deep and intimate level with the person he counsels; there must be a healthy detachment. We also see here that the Christ was very much aware of the mechanics of psychology which are usually and unfortunately attributed exclusively to our century.

One need not be a student of mundane psychology to understand any of this. It is far deeper and far more effective than any psychology taught in universities. It is connected to the spirit.

# NUMBER THIRTY-SEVEN

*Jesus says: "A city built on a high mountain, and which is strong, it is not possible that it should fall, and it cannot be hidden!"*

Building a strong city on a high mountain corresponds to building on ethical and spiritual grounds. To what extent is your life built on ethical and spiritual grounds? To what extent is your life built on the seeking of approval? How many of the decisions you have made in your life are merely the result of wanting to please somebody or to conform to a particular trend?

To the degree your life is built on a low mountain and is weak, to that degree it will fall, whether you hide it or whether you show it off. However, building in accordance to the soul plan (the Higher Self plan) results in a structure that is indestructible. Furthermore, it cannot be hidden. It is going to be seen. And it is going to have to be reckoned with.

Take the example of Christianity itself. It was built on very high principles and was started on an extraordinarily strong base. In spite of the fact that at the time of the death of Christ there were no followers—all disciples denied Him—Christianity emerged as an extremely powerful world religion. The fact that Christianity was underground for a couple of centuries did not deter its greatness. In the end it had to be seen clearly and reckoned with. The Roman Empire tried to destroy it.

Instead, it was itself destroyed and replaced by a system that was more Christian than Roman. Today, Rome is known more for the Holy Roman See, the Vatican, than for being the capital of Italy. In Italy are to be found cities that have a great deal more importance than Rome; however, there is only one Vatican, there is only one Vicar of Christ and he resides in Rome.

The same can be said about great world discoveries which in the beginning are always repressed because they bring unwelcome change which constitutes a threat to humanity's line of least resistance. Take, for instance, the discovery of the way the solar system works. When Copernicus came out with this discovery—that the Earth turned around the sun and not vice versa—it was as difficult for the Catholic Church to accept it as was earlier the notion that the Earth was a globe and not a flat disc with Jerusalem at its center. The Church did everything it could do to repress this new knowledge, including persecuting those who taught it. At the same time the church was one of the first beneficiaries of those discoveries since they helped pinpoint with greater precision the times of the Christian holidays. In spite of secretly using the new astronomical knowledge, the Catholic church was condemning it on the outer level. However, the new discoveries were built on the high mountain of bold and honest innovative thinking, on the high mountain of the purity of the Instinct of Enquiry which is divine. They cannot be destroyed. And no matter how severely or brutally they are repressed, at some point or other, they will be revealed.

Consider now your Higher Self, your innermost self, your innermost thoughts, feelings, task, etc. It is no use being ashamed of them. Sooner or later they will be revealed as the high mountain that has to be reckoned with. You must accomplish your task, however unpleasant it seems to be at first and however threatening it seems to be to your papier-mâché structures built on obtaining approval and on false needs.

# NUMBER THIRTY-EIGHT

*Jesus says: "What thou hearest with thine ear, and the other ear, proclaim from the rooftops! For no-one lights a lamp and puts it under a bushel or in a hidden place: but he puts it on the lamp-stand so that all who come in or go out should see the light."*

"What thou hearest with thine ear, and with the other ear": obviously the Christ is talking about what you hear with your inner ear, which is your guidance, that which comes from your innermost self. It is this that needs to be proclaimed from the rooftops. This constitutes your light.

It is folly to try to hide a lighted lamp under a bushel. It will set your life on fire. If you try to hide your light, you will be consumed by disaster and crisis. Conversely, any disaster and crisis that you have encountered can only have one cause to it—the hiding of your light under the papier-mâché of your city built on low ground. (See commentary Number Thirty-Seven.)

What is being heard from the inside, whatever light is being given to you from the inside, must be made available to anyone who wants to see it. The light given you is to illuminate the way for others. Show your innermost self to everybody. Shout what you have inside of you from the rooftops.

How can you possibly show your light to everybody without first expelling your darkness? The darkness which covers the light must come out first. Therefore, revealing the layers that cover the light must occur before the light itself can shine forth. You have already hidden your light under bushels. You have to remove the bushels. The process of passage through the lower self—the long dark tunnel, the dark night of the soul—is an inevitable undertaking. You cannot avoid it. If you think there is another way, you are very much mistaken. So join the Path and start the process of the dissolution of that which hides the light, the wax that plugs your inner ear.

# NUMBER THIRTY-NINE

*Jesus says: "If a blind man leads another blind man, both of them fall into a ditch."*

This is the oft-mentioned blind leading the blind. If you follow a false teacher, both you and your teacher are lost.

You must learn how to discriminate. And you must recognize as superiors those people who lead you. Sorry, "superior" is the word to use here; there is no other word. There are people who have achieved more than others on the Path. That makes them superiors.

There is such a thing as a spiritual hierarchy, based on spiritual development which is itself based upon one's desire and commitment to do the work, and, therefore, advance in the hierarchy—no New Age nonsense to the contrary. The New Age itself, the Age of Ceremony and Order, is the Age of the Seventh Ray, the Age of Hierarchy. There is no order without hierarchy.

Without hierarchy everybody is blind and everybody falls into the ditch. This is where we fundamentally differ from the Unitarians who are subtly trying to rationalize their destructive rebelliousness by claiming complete equality through eradicating all hierarchy.

# NUMBER FORTY

*Jesus says: "It is not possible for someone to enter the house of a strong man and do him violence if he has not tied his hands: [only] then will he plunder his house."*

If you are strong, no one can hurt you. In this exultation of strength we see the fact that Christ never exonerated or glamourized weakness. Christianity has reduced His teachings and His person to syrupy, sickly sweet aberrations of the original. He said: you have to be strong; strength is good—it is spiritual; it is intelligent; it is good will; and it is ultimately loving.

Having your hands tied is limiting your capacities. We impair our capacities by not admitting them. Then we overemphasize some at the expense of others, or we pretend that we have some when we actually do not, or while we are still in the process of developing them. To the degree that we have a lower self, to that degree we have our hands tied, and to that degree the devil then plunders our house. On the Path we know this for a fact: the existence of a lower self tendency attracts plunderers in the form of negative currents, negative spirits, negative friendships, negative relationships.

For example, I once met a lawyer who said that it was impossible to practice law honestly. In actuality, it was the dishonest aspect in him that continuously and perpetually attracted dishonest people and situations to him. Therefore, his dishonesty was his weakness, for it brought to him all the dishonest situations confirming that it was impossible to be an honest attorney. It is through this weakness, then, that he was being plundered of his own abilities. And as a result, he became a very bad lawyer, indeed.

Which hand is tied behind your back? Which ability is it that you have not developed? Consider this question from the point of view of the Seven Rays. How harmoniously are you developed? Consult my book, *Know Thyself,* and you will find therein a simple and accessible method of gauging your strengths and your weaknesses. Once you discover your weaknesses you will understand why there are so many robbers in your house, why you are attracting so many negative entities in the flesh or out of the flesh. Then you can begin doing something about it.

Note that it is not possible to tie the hands of a strong man unless he lets you. If he does, he stops being a strong man and becomes a weak one.

# NUMBER FORTY-ONE

*Jesus says: "Have no care, from morning to evening and from evening to morning, about what you shall put on."*

This saying is more complete if we consider the Oxyrinchus Papyrus which goes as follows: "...from morning to [evening and] from evening [to mor]ning, nor for [yo]ur [food] that you shall ea[t, nor for your] cloth[ing] that you shall put on. [You are mu]ch super[ior] to the lilies which grow and do [not sp]in. If you have a garment, what do you la[ck?] Who can add to your height? He himself will give you your clothing!"

This saying is addressed to those whose approach to life is a tight-fisted one; they give nothing, always are concerned about the future, always protecting themselves, and therefore, always creating cocoons of poverty no matter how rich they are. In our time, those people are the yuppies who think of nothing else but their upward mobility, of their accumulations of money, of houses, of status, of "deals."

In this saying, the Christ urges us to squander ourselves into our lives and trust that if we abundantly give we will abundantly receive. He compares us to the lilies. They need not think of what they are going to wear, they are beautiful in and by themselves. They are content with what they come into life with and busily go about completing their task.

To what extent does this concern you? To what extent do you care about your address, the brand of clothes you wear, the make or model of another's car? How much do you judge yourself and others from this very narrow perspective? As a result of all of this counting and comparing, you never allow yourself to explode from within, scattering your pollen all over the universe.

Very specifically examine the number of pairs of shoes you have, the clothes you hoard, the car you drive, the amount of space occupied by clutter and the amount of space unused in the place where you dwell, etc. Carry it into what you waste. How wasteful are you? How much food do you waste; how much gas, how much atmosphere, how much money? Carry this study to very precise levels and you will learn a lot about yourself. You will also get a sense of how infinitely abundant the universe is and you will stop being so concerned about your little safety and security.

If you carry this study to the emotional level we can draw a parallel between the amount of clothes you have to the number of masks you harbour. How concerned are you about the way what you say will appear to somebody? How affected is your communication with other people? How natural are you? Behind this level of mask exists that which you hoard. "I am not going to say this because I may lose 'emotional capital' from this particular person or in this particular situation." How strongly do you believe that if you conceal the truth about yourself and you present yourself as somebody you are not that you will have more clout, that it is going to get you ahead of others or ahead of the game? Politicians, for example, talk about political capital. They are concerned they might lose political capital with a particular group of constituents if they reveal either something about themselves or an opinion they have about something. For instance, if they want votes from a community that has leftist tendencies, they will conceal their conservatism and vice versa.

You see this clearly in politicians, I assure you that you

are doing the same thing here and now with your boss, with your family, with your friends, with everybody else. See if you can discover it on a subtle level. "From morning to evening and evening to morning" you are concerned with your professional, personal, family, monetary, social capital.

# NUMBER FORTY-TWO

*His disciples say to him: "On what day wilt thou appear to us, and what day shall we see thee?" Jesus says: "When you strip yourselves without being ashamed, when you take off your clothes and lay them at your feet like little children and trample on them! Then [you will become] children of Him who is living, and you will have no more fear."*

The disciples' question refers to their desire to have God come to them. God does not just appear to you. He is already there. The Christ tells them what they must do in order to be able to see God. It is the individual who must develop the capacity to see Him. In effect, you must find God since God has already found you. This is very much in accordance with our belief system.

In this saying the Christ also describes what it is that we have to do to see Him. We must shed our clothes, i.e., our masks, our pretenses, our glamours, our desire for approval, all the phoniness and dishonesties that we have accumulated. Doing it "without being ashamed" refers again to one of our beliefs, that shame is a yardstick to unresolved problems, to self-realization, and therefore, to the ability to see God and be at-one with Him. We are not only ashamed of what is negative in us, we are also hugely ashamed of who we really are underneath our clothes, i.e., we are ashamed of our Higher Self.

Check it out within yourself. You are ashamed of the best in you, that which is most personal, your innermost self. Your shame to love, for example is expressed through your shame to need, your shame to pray, and your shame to be humble. You have deeply betrayed your loving side, preferring instead to develop a persona of hardness, toughness, or indifference.

Not only must you take off your clothes without being ashamed but you have to "lay them at your feet like little children and trample on them." This means that the clothes you shed—the glamours, the masks, the seeking of approval—must be completely destroyed, so they no longer have the power they used to have when you thought you could not live without them, that you could not do anything or go anywhere without wearing those falsehoods. They have to be crumpled at your feet and you have to be able to joyously trample on them.

If you do this, "you will become like little children of Him who is living." God is the only entity Who is completely and totally living. We are partially dead. To the degree that we become alive, to that degree we get close to Him Who is life.

And last but not least, "you will have no more fear." Fear is the result of wearing masks, of wearing clothes, of wearing pretenses; fear is a direct consequence of shame. If you are ashamed of something you repress it. Repression creates an unconscious. The existence of the unknown (the unconscious) is the only reason fear exists. If you knew all about yourself, if you had total self-knowledge, you would not be afraid. Total consciousness brings total at-onement with God. Fear is only there because you are afraid of the unknown. The unknown exists only because you have created an unconscious.

A note about the first sentence of this saying: "On what day wilt thou appear to us?" Are they asking on what day Christ will appear to them, or are they are asking on what day God will appear to them? Are they equating Christ with

God? Is Christ God?

In the first place, it does not matter. For them and for us, Christ is elevated enough to be God. For us and for them, reaching Him is reaching God. This immediately excludes the necessity for religious wars, spending our energies fighting to decide whether Christ is God, or Christ is less than God, etc. Who are we to know and why should it matter so much? Christ and God both would much rather we spend our energy developing ourselves and being kind to our brothers and sisters on Earth.

In the second place, we at The Church of the Path® believe that there is indeed a difference between Christ and God. Let's not be totally simplistic about the nature of both as was necessary two thousand, four thousand or six thousand years ago. We believe as the Tibetan does, that Christ is an entity who went through incarnations on Earth and who took initiation along with His brother the Buddha in Atlantean times. Jesus, on the other hand, is a Master of Wisdom who took His initiation as a Master much later than did the Christ. He was chosen to create a body in which the Christ could manifest. He "carried" the Christ during His incarnation on Earth two thousand years ago.

In terms of the Christ's Sonship to God, we need to get into the nature of God. There is an entity by the name of Sanat Kumara who is for planet Earth the Godhead, the Ancient of Days, the One Initiator. In that sense the Christ and the Hierarchy work for Him and He resides in Shamballa with other Masters. There is another entity who is also the "Godhead" for the solar system, if we are to speak in those terms. Carried infinitely to the level of creation there is an entity, "The One About Whom Naught May Be Said," who is ultimately God and who is indeed personified and whose nature is in every iota of creation. Naught may be said about Him, not because it is forbidden but because it is impossible. What can you say about a being who is so exalted and whose existence is evolved beyond our imagination and whose presence is in every aspect of creation?

# NUMBER FORTY-THREE

*Jesus says: "You have desired many times to hear these words which I say to you, but you could not find anyone else from whom to hear them. The days will come when you will seek me, and when you will not find me."*

When we first hear the truth, we realize that we have deeply desired for a very long time to hear it and that at some level we have always known about it.

Do not take your teacher or the teachings that come through him or her for granted. You are privileged to be around the dispensation of these teachings for a limited amount of time.

The ebb and flow of the universe allows channels to be open at certain times and closed at others. This also permits for times of testing. When the channel is closed what do you do? Have you had the wisdom to develop enough so as to make your own decisions and be your own guide? I was tested in that respect. So will you be.

We are not saying that there is only one valid set of teachings. To each his own—you may need a particular set of teachings, I may need another. It is the same process when discovering one's task.

You hear, for instance, of eminent composers deciding to become musicians because they heard somebody play an instrument in a particular way or because they went to the opera at an early age. The moment they find what they want to follow there is a deep sense of recognition.

This process of recognition demonstrates that the soul is a seed. Within the soul exists a condition that is deeply fulfilled at the point of recognition. At that moment we have the feeling that we had longed for this for a long time, that we had even repressed that longing because we were convinced that what we sought was unobtainable.

When we finally find the teaching or the task we are very happy. It is a coming home to a place that we have always known but for a while we had forgotten that it existed.

# NUMBER FORTY-FOUR

*Jesus says: "The Pharisees and the scribes have taken the keys of knowledge and hidden them: they have not entered, and neither have they permitted [entry] to those who wished to enter. But you, be prudent as serpents and simple as doves!"*

This saying describes the process of monopolizing knowledge and wisdom. If you study any dispensation, it is at first given freely and openly, then insecure individuals take hold of it, declare it their own private possession and exclude others from it. By doing this they take the keys of knowledge and hide them; however, they themselves *do not enter*, i.e., they do not possess the knowledge they are trying to hide from others. If they did they would not want to hide it, they would not have to control it, they would share it freely. Because they do not have it, they have to hide it.

There is another angle to this. If the Pharisees and the scribes entered the Hall of Knowledge, they would discover their mistakes, they would be confronted with their negativities, they would have to face the necessity of change. However, in doing so, they would lose their position as high, mighty and learned—their phoniness and spiritual aridity would be exposed; everyone would recognize them for what they really are. So they have not entered.

Furthermore, they do not permit entry to those who wish to go in; these people remain in ignorance, in obedient numbness. In this context, what is the Vatican hiding from the rest of the world by concealing the abundant number of papyri and manuscripts hidden in its vaults? The same question applies to all other hermetic societies.

Christ advised His disciples to be prudent as serpents so as not to incur the destructive wrath and jealousy of those Pharisees and scribes who envied them for their proximity to the Christ and for the fact that that proximity had given them so much knowledge. When Christ taught in the form of parables He was being as prudent as a serpent. Indeed, He was sinuously trying to find answers that would not get Him in trouble. People continuously asked the Christ trick questions that would tempt Him to lose His cool and hook into these people's negative intent. I am afraid that the Christ Himself did not follow His own advice, it was not very prudent a serpent of Him to enter Jerusalem, to overturn the tables and to have made Himself available for arrest and crucifixion.

"Simple as doves" means simply applying spiritual material to the problems of everyday life. Any truth that cannot be applied to your problems here and now is not only worthless but regressive. It is useless to engage in the sophistry of the scribes and Pharisees with their disputes about the extent of knowledge, the nature of knowledge, the keys of knowledge, etc. The highest form of knowledge is in your hands. It exists in your ability to connect that which is within you with that which is occurring in your life. Your task is simply to bridge that gap. If you do, then you will coo and you will love and you will fly as do the doves.

The Dark Ages, medieval times, saw the apogee of "Christian" faith. These ages were dark because the priests and the scribes had hidden the keys of knowledge. Not only had the Catholic Church concealed from the populace the Keys to the Kingdom but they also idealized ignorance, euphemistically calling it simplicity. They chose to follow

Tertullian who said that because something did not make sense it was divine. Of course, what he meant was we should keep our minds open to the wonders of God's creation even though we do not understand them. This is the kernel of truth in his teaching. However, when this teaching is used to advocate concealing knowledge, it highlights the intent of the medieval church fathers to exert their power over the faithful and take advantage of them by keeping them ignorant.

The other extreme of knowledge—gnosis—also went too far. The Gnostics indeed wasted themselves in incredibly complicated and nonsensical considerations about the structure of the universe with all of its hierarchies and Mother Goddess at the center, etc. However, even there is to be found a kernel of truth—the existence of a hierarchy and of God immanent, God in everything and everyone. This was seen as dangerous by the Catholic Church and repressed. It is the aspect knowledge, knowledge as a principle, i.e., the Third Ray.

A wonderful advocate of knowledge who also believed in reincarnation, as well as life before and after death, was Origen. His teachings are usually contrasted to Tertullian. An act of his that he later very much regretted was his own castration. He castrated himself so as to better follow the teachings of the church. Of course, he then realized how unnatural that was. In spite of the fact that he has been much forgotten by the Catholic Church, Origen and his philosophy was a lot closer to the truth than the church.

A note in their defense: there was a time when knowledge had to be reserved for the few who were wise enough to use it. This was when the kings were enlightened guides of the race—this was during the times of Atlantis.

However, in our civilization, and definitely during our New Age it is time to open the doors and let fresh air into all of these heretofore hidden places. The fact that this Gospel of Thomas was found now is no accident. Humanity is ready to rediscover the repressed aspects of the Christ's teachings, the lost teachings of the Christ.

# NUMBER FORTY-FIVE

*Jesus says: "A vine shoot was planted outside the Father. It did not grow strong: it will be plucked up from the root and it will perish."*

Anything planted outside the Father will not grow correctly. It will not be strong; it will be weak; it will be distorted; it must be plucked up from the roots and replanted. Anything that is built outside of truth, love, and personal responsibility will have to be destroyed. To the degree that, in our lives, we have built anything outside of the Father, to that degree it will have to undergo this process of uprooting and death.

Since no teachings in our relative world are absolute. At some point or another, they will all be uprooted and destroyed. There is no way that anything can be totally planted in the Father in this three-dimensional reality.

Therefore, we have to accept and expect continuous and perpetual change. We have to be willing to continuously uproot and dissolve the places in us that have misconceptions, the ways that we have built outside of the Father, the Absolute.

# NUMBER FORTY-SIX

*Jesus says: "To him who has in his hand, [more] will be given. But from him who has not, [even] the little he has will be taken away!"*

The Christ is *not* saying that the universe is bad. On the contrary, this is a demonstration of the universe's generosity.

There are those who are aware that they have and are generous with what they have. However poor they may be, they are generous, they can "have in their hand." To these people more will be given. More will be given to those who have.

If many people were willing to do this for their society, then everybody would be rich and everybody would have more and more and more, ad infinitum. It is the attitude of acting as if we do not have, as if we have to keep the little that we have and jealously guard it by giving it to our children, that it gets taken away and that turns it negative.

To him who has not, notwithstanding how rich he actually is in goods, he is poor in spirit and in consciousness. He does not share what he has; he does not put to use what he has; he does not involve his possessions or his talents in the workings of humanity, for humanity's sake. By definition this person is "poor." He will lose whatever he has.

Here we enter into the realm of possessions. What is the meaning of possessing something? In the last analysis, it is relative. Do you own the trees on your property? Yes, you do, but yet again, no, you do not. God made them, God owns them. They belong to nature. You are simply their custodian for the time that you are around. You should treat those possessions and everything else you "own" as such, as being a temporary custodian of them.

Think, for instance, about inheritance. This is a process by which someone receives something for which he has not worked. The corruption that comes from this is immeasurable. When this is perpetuated generation after generation, an entire civilization is corrupted. There are many historical examples of this. Consider, for example, the kings of France. Louis XIV knew poverty. As a young king under his mother's regency, he went through bad times. This is what made him value his position as king. Because of this, and in spite of his excesses as king, his reign is the golden age of France, innovations in just about every field occurred through the French.

However, his successor and great grandson, Louis XV, was a very poor king, indeed. He is the one who said, "After me, the deluge." Indeed, he took for granted his wealth and his position. He never wanted to have any discomfort whatsoever, never wanted to confront anybody, and never wanted to take responsibility for anything that was happening to his country or anywhere else. He was a terrible judge of character and managed to push away from him many people who could have made of his reign and of his person vehicles of progress, achievement and great satisfaction

In turn, Louis XV's grandson, Louis XVI was even less effectual, though less corrupt. He it is who took the brunt of the years of corruption of his predecessors by being beheaded and incurring the French Revolution. Take another example, the Roman emperors. The first ones were very capable and had a relatively high sense of morality. Indeed,

Julius Caesar and his nephew Octavian, later Augustus, were a lot better than the ones who followed them, Caligula, Nero, etc.

Unless someone is of great spiritual development, if he is born to a position of riches and power, he will be corrupted by that very same wealth and the power. We have seen it before and we will see it again.

When a person receives something that he has not earned, he sinks into poverty. He is debilitated. He does not feel that he is capable or worthy of earning anything. He develops a desire to be given to for the rest of his days. He has neither a reason to develop a task and to follow it nor a motive to give, believing that anything he gives he cannot get back since the little he was given will never be given to him again.

The process of leaving money to children is a course of impoverization. It demonstrates a lack of trust in the universe. Keeping it in the family is a euphemism for keeping it in one's own pocket after one's death. It is reminiscent of the superstition of the pharaohs which kept Egypt in poverty for untold centuries. An enlightened government should be able to take care of this and create the necessary funds for education and medicine to be universal. The privilege of good schooling and proper medical care should not be the exclusive property of those who have the money.

# NUMBER FORTY-SEVEN

*Jesus says: "You must be [as] passers-by!"*

In other words, be in the world, but not of the world. Do not develop ties to materialism. Here is, of course, the connection between Number Forty-Seven and Number Forty-Six. Gently and effortlessly live your life, accomplishing your task, helping people and enjoying yourself.

If you live your life lightly and elegantly, without demand, without despair, without condemning, without condoning, nature will transport you and you will walk on water, life will be lived through you.

# NUMBER FORTY-EIGHT

*His disciples said to him: "Who art thou, who tellest us these things?" "By the things that I tell you, do you not recognize who I am? But you yourselves have become like the Jews: they like the tree and detest the fruit, they like the fruit and detest the tree!"*

What His disciples asked Him calls for the assertion of His authority.

The disciples are challenging the Christ's authority. Indeed, who was He? Nobody ever officially appointed Him; He was not teaching anything that was taught Him by anyone in the body; He had no credentials. How dare He then present them with all of these unpalatable sayings that go to the core of their being and show them aspects of themselves that they do not want to see?

My authority has been challenged as well. Who am I to start The Church of the Path®? I have been asked this many times. I once filled the pulpit at a Unitarian Church in Brownsville, Texas. Significantly, an ex-rabbi asked me, "Who are you to tell us these things?" My response was that it did not matter who I was; I further remarked to him that the intensity of his response demonstrated to me that there was something in what I said that touched him deeply and that he did not want to look at it. Every dispensation encounters this difficulty. After all, who was that drunken Mohammed when he started teaching? Who was Buddha, who was Milarepa, etc.? Nobody is forcing anyone to be anybody's follower. The Christ goes one step further. He urges His disciples to recognize in Him their teacher.

One forgets so very often that the responsibility to find the teacher lies entirely with the student. The teacher's responsibility is simply to teach. If he is dumb enough to try to seduce you into accepting his teachings he is a bad teacher. If you are dumb enough to want to be seduced and to want to be desired, then you will attract the wrong teacher. But if you find yourself saying, "Who are you to tell me this?," then you are probably facing somebody who is, in one way or another, your teacher. Otherwise you would not have that reaction.

It is the same with guidance. Any inner guidance that is valid will confront you on your lower self. If it flatters you, if it tells you things that you want to hear, then 99.44% of the time it is false; you are being seduced and you want to be seduced. The art of finding the right teacher goes hand in hand with the art of finding, admitting and dissolving that in you which is so unpalatable and so difficult.

Does the finding of the right teacher depend on the amount of negativities you have resolved within yourself? No, it does not. It depends on your intent to dissolve them, your desire to dissolve them. The desire alone will make you a candidate for the right teacher. Indeed, the Christ was a lot more a teacher to thieves, scoundrels, prostitutes, than he was to "good" citizens.

Do you have to search forever, be a seminar buff, a workshop addict to find the right teacher? No. In fact, seminar buffs and workshop addicts escape the right teachings through multiplicity. They may have found the right teacher and were not able to recognize him. They are escaping that within themselves which needs to be worked out. More often than not, the person who is ready to find his teacher does not have long to look. His unconscious leads him to the teacher through strange ways. God works in wondrous ways.

When the disciple is ready the Master appears. Seek and you shall find. When there is longing in your soul that is genuine and pure, i.e., connected to nature, your fulfillment is at hand.

*** 

He admonishes them about having become like the Jews. In the days that this gospel was given, the Jews liked the tree [God] but detested the fruit [His Son].

On the other hand the Jews liked the fruit when it was given earlier, i.e., in the dispensations of Moses and the Ten Commandments during the Age of Aries, but detested the tree by ignoring the fact that God was to send a Messiah who needed to be recognized by the Jews.

This wishy-washy process is familiar to all of us. Everyone goes through this. It is the process of disconnecting cause from effect, the tree from the fruit and the fruit from the tree.

Our task is to connect the fruit to the tree, cause to effect. Our fruits are the manifestations and circumstances of our lives. The tree is that in us which created those manifestations. Do not be like the Jews who forget one and favour the other.

See also the commentary of Number Ninety-Four.

# NUMBER FORTY-NINE

*Jesus says: "He who has blasphemed the Father will be forgiven, and he who has blasphemed the Son will be forgiven: but he who has blasphemed the Holy Spirit will not be forgiven either on earth or in heaven."*

The Holy Spirit here means the aspect of Deity that is related to Mother/Matter. This is the aspect whereby everything that exists is God-infused. The concept of the Holy Spirit has been lost to us. It is the concept of the all-pervasive divine Mother God, the experiential, manifest aspect of Deity, Ray Three.

Blasphemy of the Holy Spirit is experiential blasphemy. It is the deep, all-encompassing blasphemy. Blasphemy of the Father or of the Son is blasphemy of a particular entity. It is not all-encompassing. By blasphemy on the experiential level, I mean wrong living, living in accordance to distortion, living against God, against nature. We all do that and to the extent we do that we are condemned, not forgiven. The part that remains in negativity remains unforgiven.

This means that we have to take responsibility for the consequences of our negativity and its inherent existence in us at the point when we blaspheme. It perforce has consequences and those consequences have to be resolved.

The karma that they create must be paid for. This is true on earth or in heaven, i.e., on the outer and on the inner levels, on the level of manifestation as well as on the level of thought and feeling.

Here the Christ is trying to confirm the fact that He is not trying to promote a personality cult. You may not be a believer of His and still make it to the Kingdom of Heaven. You may not even be a believer of the Father and still make it to the Kingdom of Heaven. Many atheists, in my opinion, will make it to the Kingdom of Heaven a lot sooner than many devout Christians, as they like to call themselves.

It is important to be forgiven because it opens for you the gates of Paradise, at-onement with God, which is your task. Not being forgiven means continuously going against nature, the will of God. That in itself is blaspheming the Holy Spirit.

"But he who has blasphemed the Holy Spirit will not be forgiven either on earth or in heaven." Here the Christ is demonstrating a very advanced teaching that goes beyond the Age of Pisces, right into the Age of Aquarius. He asserts that everything which is true in heaven is also true on Earth. Earth is very much a part of heaven, only we have made it what it is, disconnected from heaven and to that extent miserable. Negativity will create misery on Earth as well as in heaven. Here, again, heaven means the inner levels, the levels of thought and feeling, as opposed to the level of manifestation.

Death does not liberate us from negativity. We take with us when we die our negativities and have as a task to work them out later in another incarnation or in another situation.

# NUMBER FIFTY

*Jesus says: "Grapes are not gathered from thistles, and figs are not gathered from thorns: they do not give fruit! [...a] good man brings out of his barn what is good, but a wicked man brings out of his wicked barn—which is in his heart—evil [things], and from them he sows evil, because [they are] evil [things that] he brings out of the abundance of his heart."*

You cannot create good from bad. This obvious message is abundantly clear from these words of the Christ. However, a much deeper process is also described. It is familiar to those of us who are on the Path.

In order to best understand it, follow this sequence on an inner level as well as on an outer level:

1. As an infant you demanded total and unconditional love from everybody, particularly your parents.

2. This desire is fundamentally good since it seeks God's love which is infinite and absolute. However, since it is experienced on this three-dimensional relative plane, it is bound to encounter frustration.

3. Having encountered frustration it constructs wrong conclusions, perhaps so as to deal with the pain of injustice, the greatest pain that humanity can possibly experience since it demonstrates that God does not exist. So, for example, in order to explain my mother's or my father's withholding or cruelty or lack of giving I start associating all women or all men with withholding or cruelty. This then begins the formation of the lower self, the negative aspect within me, the thistles and the thorns within me.

4. Deep down inside of me I conclude that in order to be

strong I have to be cruel, if I am loving I am going to be rejected, and if I am generous I am going to be taken advantage of, etc. I, therefore, decide in order to "make it" in this world, I must be cruel, greedy, ungiving, ruthless, etc.

5. At the same time I may not have obtained my parents' and society's love, but have instead settled for obtaining their approval. This also is a thistle or a thorn that I develop within myself—the seeking of outside approval rather than the search for the total and unconditional love of God on the inner level.

6. I, therefore, adopt an attitude and a behavioural pattern that appears to be good, lawful, worthy of approval, generous, loving, amiable, good willed. I even develop skills for the sake of approval, such as intelligence, manners, musical ability, etc.

These are not positive aspects; they are pseudo-positive. They are the pseudo-figs and the pseudo-grapes that I have gathered. They cannot and never will be good in and by themselves since they originate from the bad (my desire for approval).

\*\*\*

The second part of the saying refers to the same thing. The "wicked barn" in the evil man's heart is the place that we call the lower self in which the freezes, the negativities, the wrong conclusions were formed. No matter how abundantly we give, if this giving, this love, this goodwill has as its origin the evil of the lower self, if it is motivated by approval seeking or by greed, or to cover up any of these negativities, these gifts will sow evil however good they are; not only will they be for naught, but they will bring unhappiness and misery for everyone concerned.

If you contrast this with the necessity to bring out and reveal the worst in you so as to have it become the best you find the following differences between the former and the latter:

Bringing out the worst in you will demonstrate that the worst leads to unhappiness and misery. This truth will be understood a lot sooner than if you bring out the pseudo-best in you in an attempt to hide the worst.

For example, if I pretend to be loving while behind it hiding a cruel intent—possessiveness or enslavement—I will create great unhappiness without ever cleansing my cruelty. If I act blatantly cruelly I will create unhappiness but at least everyone, including myself, will know that the unhappiness has been created due to my cruelty. Since I am naturally a pleasure and happiness seeking individual, being a child of God, I will want to purify the cruelty since it is bringing such evident unhappiness. So, blatant cruelty is preferable to cruelty masked by love.

The best scenario is the one in which I reveal my cruelty without acting it out, knowing that I am cruel and wanting to cleanse it. This process of extricating the negative within us is practiced on our Path, in our groups, in our lessons, in our prayers, in our process. The cruelty thus exposed and revealed is transformed into its positive component—vigour, energy, potency. So will every single aspect that has turned negative be transformed into its positive component when it is revealed to the light. Cruelty will become vigour and energy, fear will become love, cunning will become wisdom, conflict will become harmony.

# NUMBER FIFTY-ONE

*Jesus says: "From Adam to John the Baptist, among those who have been born of women, there is none greater than John the Baptist! But for fear that the eyes [of such a one] should be lost I have said: He who among you shall be the small[est] shall know the Kingdom and be higher than John!"*

Let's study this in three parts:

1. "From Adam to John the Baptist, among those who have been born of women, there is none greater than John the Baptist." This is quite a statement in and by itself. John the Baptist is, therefore, greater than any other human being born since the beginning of time. He is greater than Moses, he is greater than Buddha. The corresponding place in the Scriptures is Luke 7:28, "I tell you, among those born of women none is greater than John; yet he who is least in the kingdom of God is greater than he."

We must remember that John the Baptist was concerned with purification. In modern parlance, his preaching of repentance means purification. When you take responsibility for your lower self, when you reveal the worst in you so as to have it become the best, you are actually doing what John the Baptist recommended that you do. He was the Baptist because he purified people through water, which is initiation. The Christ here simply underlines the primordial importance of purification.

2. "But for fear that the eyes of such a one should be lost I have said": this is totally omitted from the "scriptures" mentioned above. What the Christ is saying is do not let what I am telling you go to your head. Do not inflate your

ego with the notion that you are better than anybody else, that you are the center of the universe.

Why interpret the meaning of "but for fear that the eyes of such a one should be lost I have said" as "do not let what I am telling you go to your head?" I think that the Christ is here making a remark for the benefit both of John the Baptist as well as those who are listening to Him. He is saying that although John the Baptist is the greatest, you can attain his greatness and go even further by "being the smallest." Let not greatness inflate your ego. Let it not "lose your eyes," i.e., cloud your vision, which should always be towards the process of purification, a humbling process. Remember that "greatness" in the worldly sense can be confused with goodness and with the capacity to enter the kingdom of God.

3. "He who among you shall be the smallest shall know the Kingdom and be higher than John," reminds us that it is by being small, i.e., without baggage, that we will make it to the kingdom of God. Making it to the kingdom of God will make us higher than was John during his days on Earth. This demonstrates that everybody has a lower self. As long as you are in the body you must go through a system of purification. When you no longer need to incarnate then you have made it to the kingdom of God and you are indeed higher than John and higher than anybody else who still needs to incarnate on Earth as John the Baptist himself had to do.

So you become the greatest by being the smallest, by being able to go through the eye of the needle, free of your lower self baggage. The process of purification which is the sine qua non condition for being on the Path has been totally omitted from that which has been erroneously called the "scriptures."

# NUMBER FIFTY-TWO

*Jesus says: "It is not possible for a man to ride two horses, nor to draw two bows. And it is not possible for a servant to serve two masters: otherwise he will honour the one and the other will treat him harshly! Never does a man drink old wine and desire at the same instant to drink new wine; new wine is not poured into old wine-skins, in case they should burst, and old wine is not poured into new wine-skins, in case it should be spoiled. An old piece of cloth is not sown onto a new garment, for a tear would result."*

In this saying, the Christ calls us to unity, highlighting and exposing the fallacy of duality. Where is it in your life that you ride two horses? Look for the places that have sought approval. Your unquenchable thirst for approval has led you to agree with contradictory theories, with accepting belief systems that you have not thought through, and therefore, with creating enormous contradictions within yourself. You have impaired your integrity by "riding two horses." Here, He is instructing you to think for yourself, to reconnect with every single element of faith or knowledge that you have accepted without questioning. Discover your own truth. If you are wrong, you will find that out yourself, experientially, and you will then come up with the truth for yourself and by yourself.

The worst possible thing that can happen to you in this respect is to have accepted a belief, true in and by itself, without thinking it through. Anything that you have not thought through, you will have to reject. At some point in your life you will become its enemy simply because it is not your truth; it is somebody else's. You have acquired it for their approval. When you realize that you have sold out to that person by accepting that truth from them, you will have to rebel if you have any integrity—and fundamentally you have integrity since you are God in your deepest possible self. In rejecting this truth, you will hurt, you will create unhappiness and pain—until the time comes when you realize that it was true after all. Then you will have found it out for yourself. Therefore, you will never have to rebel against this truth again. You will integrate it, accept it, use it. It is yours and it is yours naturally.

"...nor to draw two bows." The drawing of the bow corresponds to goal setting, to direction. Indeed, this is connected to the sign of Sagittarius. Riding two horses is a more receptive allegory, i.e., being transported by two powerful forces which you cannot control. Drawing two bows refers more specifically to you being in control and setting your own goals. The Christ here shows us the impossibility of pursuing two different directions at the same time. If, as I have explained above, you have allowed yourself to believe contradictory things for the sake of approval, you will also be tempted to set goals and conduct your life—draw bows—in as many different directions as you have sought approval. And you will be torn apart.

"And it is not possible for a servant to serve two masters." This is a warning to hypocrites, to those who compromise. One cannot compromise with the truth. There is only one truth and you must find it within yourself. There is only one religion and that is your religion. There is only one set of beliefs and it is the one that you discover yourself. Any deviation from that will lead you to serving two masters—at least two. The result will be that no matter how much you capitulate to these masters, they will treat you harshly.

"Never does a man drink old wine and desire at the same instant to drink new wine." You cannot sit in your organized churches drinking the old and obsolete and stale and musty and distorted teachings while at the same time desiring new ones, desiring to find your True Self, your soul, etc. You will destroy yourself as well as those institutions that you hold onto so tightly. Also, you cannot make love to your wife while having fantasies about other women. You cannot make love to your husband while having fantasies about other men. So, how do we solve this problem? We solve it by candidly admitting that there is something wrong in what we are doing here and now. We solve it by seeking the truth wherever we are and by honestly confronting and exposing untruth wherever we find it, whether inside ourselves or outside of ourselves. Do you have the guts to tell your churches, your synagogues, your mosques, your temples that what they are teaching is obsolete and that it has absolutely no reference to modern life unless you twist the teachings and bend them over backwards? If you do not do that, you will never find the truth; you will continue to cultivate falsehood and you will be a hypocrite.

Conversely, "new wine is not poured into old wine skins in case they should burst." This reminds me of conventional religions' attempt to be infused with teachings and practices that belong to the New Age dispensation. Indeed, a lot of those who call themselves Christian have formed movements, such as the Curseo movement in the Episcopal Church, which are trying out growth processes that had heretofore been the practices of New Age spiritual communities. It will not work. It is new wine in old skins. The old skins will burst from the infusion of the new wine. It has no integrity. Faced with the powerful material coming from New Age dispensations, the old skins will indeed burst; the old structures will be destroyed and replaced by new ones, the new religions, this religion that we are preaching.

"...and old wine is not poured into new wine-skins, in case it should be spoiled." We are vessels, receptacles into which is poured information, guidance, material, faith, etc. If you pour old teachings into new skins—children or young people—you will spoil them. You will damage them. An entire generation of young people has recently been damaged by the resurgence of conservatism and "churchianity"—the distortion of Christianity—in the 1980s and the 1990s.

"An old piece of cloth is not sewn onto a new garment, for a tear would result." This reminds me of the attempt of some hypocritical New Age organizations to cater to old time religion for the sake of approval, for the sake of not being seen as a rabble rouser, etc. They will even go so far as to adopt for their name something that is reminiscent of old time religion. In reality, their hypocrisy is similar to this old cloth sown on a new garment. The old cloth is the pretense of agreeing with old time religion and the new garment is, of course, the New Age dispensation. The tear occurs when those who still belong to the old conventional religions discover the scheme and feel cheated. Then the poor new garment is torn by the fanatics who discover its falsehood. This has actually happened to a community of our acquaintance which thought that it would ingratiate itself with the local populace but actually created a great deal of antagonism and alienation.

# NUMBER FIFTY-THREE

*Jesus says: "If two people are with each other in peace in the same house, they will say to the mountain: 'Move!' and it will move."*

Here again is duality being exposed and unity evoked. The two people who are with each other in peace in the same house are obviously the duality within ourselves. Duality characterizes humanity. In each one of us is a duality, usually characterized by the aspect and attributes of mother and father. Through a Path such as this one, inner unity is reached within the house, i.e., within a particular human being. When that unity is achieved, and to the degree it is achieved, unlimited powers will be available to the individual who will then "be able to move mountains."

# NUMBER FIFTY-FOUR

*Jesus says: "Blessed are the solitary and the elect, for you will find the Kingdom! Because you have issued from it, you will return to it again."*

The "solitary" here is the person who has become one, whole. Solitary as opposed to dualized.

Fundamentally, we are elect. Within ourselves there is a place that is at-one and that seeks the kingdom of God. Everyone is a potential "elect." Only he needs to become "solitary" and then he will be able to find the kingdom of God.

Why? "Because you have come from it" and to it you must return. There is really no choice in the matter. Eventually, everyone will make it and everyone will be elect.

# NUMBER FIFTY-FIVE

*Jesus says: "If people ask you: "Where have you come from?" tell them: 'We have come from the Light, from the place where the Light is produced [...] outside itself [or: of itself?]. It [...] until they show (?) [...] their image.' If someone says to you: 'What are you?' say: 'We are the sons and we are the elect of the living Father.' If [people] ask you: 'What sign of your Father is in you?' tell them: 'It is a movement and a rest.'"*

Before we launch into its explanation, here is the way I believe it should be written. "If people ask you: 'Where have you come from?' tell them: 'We have come from the Light, from the place where the Light is produced of and by itself. It shone until it manifested in us, its image.' If someone says to you: 'What are you?' say: 'We are the sons and we are the elect of the living Father.' If people ask you: 'What sign of your Father is in you?' tell them: 'It is a movement and a rest.'"

For Light to manifest in our three-dimensional reality, it must descend—it must slow its vibration. The purest forms of the manifestation of the Light are the teachers, those who usher in new dispensations. The Light, which produces itself by itself also produced us, the teachers, who spread the Light from whence we came. Anyone can become a spreader of the Light because everyone has come from the Light. Becoming the spreader of the Light is the natural consequence of the process of purification, of the Path. The Christ is urging the disciples to acknowledge that they are teachers when they talk about themselves, when they are

*A Commentary on the Gospel of Thomas*

asked "Who are you and where do you come from?"

This brings me to a warning: do not attempt purification of yourself for the wrong reasons. Understand that any and all purification processes will lead you to become an agent of the Light. The difference between growth for the right and for the wrong reasons defines the difference between psychotherapy and spiritual work. In psychotherapy, you resolve a problem. When your problem is resolved, you end psychotherapy—you take your marbles and go home. On the Path, even if you resolve all your problems, you still continue on the Path as a teacher and as a bearer of the Light. At some point or other in your process of growth and of self-actualization, you will find yourself urged to teach the material, to be an agent of the Light. If you do not heed this call, everything that you have learned and all the progress that you have achieved will turn against you. The former method uses the Light but stops at the point where the little ego is satisfied with the results. In the latter case, stopping is not a viable alternative; it is erroneous to think that you can gather your marbles and go home without any consequences. If you do, the marbles that you have gathered will become disconnected from their spiritual source and, therefore, turn negative and against you. Eventually, you become worse off than before you started.

All of the people who were at some time committed to this Path of Self-Transformation and who have left fall into this category. They reached a point where they had received so much good they knew that they must start giving, being the bearers of Light. Instead, they closed up shop, folded up their tent, believing that they could retreat and take advantage of what they had achieved. They cannot. The minute one tries to hold on to what he has achieved in such a manner, not only will he lose his achievements, but he will become the enemy of the achievements themselves.

Enter the Path knowing that it is an unending search, knowing that in the beginning it will deal with and resolve your personal problems but in the long run you will have to become a torchbearer, a teacher. Stay away from the Path if you do not understand this. Do not use the Path for psychotherapeutic reasons or else you will get burnt.

In the second part of this saying, the Christ urges the disciples to assert themselves as being the elect, being the ones chosen by the Living God, the Living Father to spread the teaching. The people ask them to demonstrate this, to give a tangible proof of this. The tangible proof is a "movement and a rest."

If you look at our material on mobility and relaxation, you will find that we say that every problem stems from an imbalance between mobility and relaxation, between movement and rest. Every single one of your distortions and of your problems, i.e., every single way that you have disconnected from nature, from God, originates from an imbalance in the rhythmic movement of nature which is mobility and relaxation.

If you know how to be active and how to be receptive at the proper times, you will have become self-actualized; you will have become elect. Also, everyone will recognize this in you, will admire you, will emulate you and will see in you a teacher by example. You cannot be a teacher except by example. Thus, as a teacher, you must have rigorously applied to yourself that which you teach to your students.

# NUMBER FIFTY-SIX

*His disciples said to him: "On what day shall rest come to those who are dead, and on what day shall the new world come?" He said to them: "This [rest] that you wait for has [already] come, and you have not recognized it."*

If rest is to come to those who are dead, then, those who are dead are disturbed or are not resting. We see here how strongly the Greek/pagan influence had taken root amongst the disciples of Christ—and by extension, the rest of Jewry at that time. Indeed, for the Jews, you simply return to dust and are resurrected on Judgment Day. However, for the Greeks, once you are dead, you wander in Hades.

"And on what day shall the new world come," refers to the new dispensation, the Age of Pisces, which was already upon them. The Age of Pisces inaugurated by the Christ and His dispensation corresponds to the Age of Aquarius, our new world, our New Age.

The Christ makes this very clear when He responds that both have already come without being recognized. Indeed, if the new dispensations are recognized when they are given, then "rest" comes. The soul is in accord with the Universal Life Force as it manifests at that particular moment in the here and now.

Those who recognized the Christ found rest within themselves, no matter what happened to them and no matter how much they were persecuted.

Those who today are open to the New Age dispensations find rest as well, since they are in accord with the form that the Universal Life Force has taken today.

Note that the word "rest", which is in brackets, does not really need to be there which then justifies my contention that the Christ answers both questions at once by saying essentially that the day of rest has come for the dead and also the new world has come.

In order to find peace, we have to live in the here and now; we must recognize the Universal Life Force as it exists in this moment. This requires submitting to a purification process such as the one we practice in our church. Other forms of purification were in existence in Christ's time. The Path and the practice of the Path were then different from what it is now.

It is interesting to find in Luke 17:20-21 a saying that much resembles the one in Thomas.

"Being asked by the Pharisees when the kingdom of God was coming, he answered them, 'The kingdom of God is not coming with signs to be observed; nor will they say, "Lo, here it is!" or "There!" for behold, the kingdom of God is in the midst of you.'"

How does conventional Christianity explain this saying? Doesn't it contradict the belief that peace can only be found out of this world? When the Christ says that you cannot tell by observation when the kingdom of God comes, isn't he contradicting the Christian belief that says (a) the Messiah has visibly appeared, and (b) that Judgment Day will be preceded by all kinds of hosannas and trumpets and seraphim? There certainly is a gap here between conventional Christianity and acceptance of process. Conventional Christianity misses the point in its oblivion to the fact that increased consciousness, increased awareness make the kingdom of God reveal itself in the here and now.

I can also see another way of looking at this in

accordance with other New Age teachings. The Christ's task was to come in and fray a passage for humanity to be liberated from the clutches of evil. His task was not merely to give us the teachings that He gave, for they can be found in other places. They contain some innovative material but not much in the last analysis. The task of Christ was to challenge the forces of darkness and to achieve in battle a major victory over them to release a passage to the superhuman kingdom.

It seems that there came a point in the history of humanity during which the prince of darkness had been so successful in tricking and tripping humanity into faltering that it became virtually impossible for anyone to make it through the astral level into the kingdom of God or into the superhuman kingdom as it is understood by us. During a council of the guides of Humanity, Christ brought this to the attention of "The Presiding One"—God—and all the others present. It was decided that they would confront the prince of darkness about that. Christ, Himself, confronted him. The prince of darkness pointed out that there was nothing that anybody in the camp of the Forces of Light could do about the situation since intervening would take away a human being's initiative in bringing about his own salvation. The Christ then asked him that if one Being of Light were to incarnate and live a life free of sins, would he then agree to do battle against the Forces of Light? The prince of darkness agreed under the condition that it be a limited battle, i.e., that the Forces of Light not invest all of their personnel in the seeking of victory. The prince of darkness knew very well that the Forces of Light were infinite and that his finite grip on this world cannot possibly win a battle against all the Forces of Light. He, therefore, requested that the ratio be

20:1—twenty soldiers of the dark forces against one soldier of the Forces of Light. Christ consented to all of these terms.

The Christ went back to the council and presented the terms that He had agreed to. He also suggested that He be the one to incarnate. This brought great consternation and worry among the Forces of Light. Nevertheless, Christ prevailed and was given the opportunity and the task to incarnate.

So He did, choosing the body of Master Jesus. The prince of darkness never knew of His identity during the entire incarnation of the Christ in the body of Jesus. The plan was very carefully devised.

If you consider the span of history that begins around 600 B.C. and ends around 600 A.D. you see in it a wide plan in the middle of which is to be found the birth of Christ. He was preceded by Buddha, who brought the Four Noble Truths. We then have the Greco-Roman period which provided roads, stability, and a *lingua franca*, ensuring the propagation of teachings to a considerable part of the world. On the more immediate level, John the Baptist preceded Him, fraying a passage of rigorous purification before His arrival.

The culmination of this dispensation came with Mohammed, who inaugurated the Islamic era in 622 A.D., with his *Higra*, or "Flight." Islam was a force that cleansed, albeit destructively, the excesses of Byzantium and of the adjacent Syrian Empire. This marks the end of the dispensation and the beginning of the Dark Ages, the worst possible times—the long, dark tunnel—of Christianity.

Christ's arrival, itself, was met with great obstacles which one by one were overcome, such as, for example, Herod's execution of all first born males during the year of His birth which precipitated the flight of His family to Egypt. The great temptations of Christ are well known through the Gospels.

They are even more convincingly explained in many passages of the *Urantia Book*. New Age teachings point out that aside from all of the difficulties that the Christ had, He was not allowed to communicate with any spirit guides. He was to come in open and mediumistic, be subject to all the temptations that flesh is heir to, and never have the benefit of spirit guides to help Him. He was to rediscover from within all of the teachings that He gave us, as well as His identity as the leader of the Hierarchy and of the Forces of Light.

All of this He successfully did. The minute He died on the cross, He wasted no time in summoning the forces that were ready to join Him in battle against darkness on the astral level. The success of His battle has ensured a passage to the kingdom of God. Now the forces of darkness must adhere to very specific conditions before they can tempt the individual. If they trespass, the Forces of Light have the right to intervene on the individual's behalf.

Think, for example, of the fact that the martyred Christians who could very easily have been extinguished as a sect finally triumphed and became the official—and fanatically bigoted—religion of the Roman Empire. Here is a specific example of the forces of darkness trespassing and being summarily dealt with by the Forces of Light. There are many, many other examples in our daily lives. There have been many examples in my own personal life of this fact.

In living a life free of sinful deeds (not free of sinful thoughts or sinful feelings; check "Why hast Thou forsaken me?"), the Christ merely won the opportunity to do battle against the forces of darkness. This battle was waged on the astral level which He entered after His body died, after the physical vehicle was relinquished.

The prince of darkness has his greatest power on the astral level. The crossing of the astral level, which is the crossing of our emotional life, brings us to the mental level where it is a lot more possible to examine our distortions and make sense of them, resolve them, thus adjusting our emotions and actions that exist below it. The battle had to be waged on the astral level so as (a) to attack the devil where he resides and (b) to leave the opportunity for humanity to do the work that needs to be done on the physical level. The fundamental, primary level of purification, remains primordially the physical. The entrance into the emotional purification comes after the Second Initiation, the entrance to the Path, purification by fire.

The darkness at midday which is described by the witnesses of Christ's death is the physical effect of His entrance into the dark world and challenging the forces of evil. The battle was waged for three days and three nights. The reappearance of the Christ after this in the form of resurrection. His appearance to us, those of us who have been fortunate enough to have experienced Him, is proof positive of His victory over the dark forces. He now has free passage in and out of this world which He claims as God's world, no longer the prince of darkness'.

"Follow Me" now has a greater significance. We follow Him on the path He has frayed for us through the dangers presented by the forces of darkness.

When the Christ says "This that you wait for has come, and you have not recognized it," He is clearly talking about the full significance of His presence in terms of the new opportunity for liberation for mankind. It is important to remember that all of this has absolutely no meaning without process. It is through a process of self-transformation and of purification that we are able to raise our consciousness to the point where we start recognizing the ever-presence of the kingdom of God. This then slowly becomes an experiential reality to the point where we become part of the kingdom of God without even leaving the body.

# NUMBER FIFTY-SEVEN

*His disciples said to him: "Twenty-four prophets spoke in Israel, and they all spoke through you!" He said to them: "You have passed over Him who is living in front of your eyes, and have spoken of the dead!"*

The twenty-four previous prophets do not bring the depth that Christ brings. He, being the greatest of them all, spoke through them and now speaks for Himself, here and now. In spite of the disciples' obvious flattery of Christ, Christ points out to them a grave, albeit, subtle problem: their need to continuously refer to the past rather than appreciate the present.

There is a Chinese proverb that says, "Man reaches for the stars above while trampling on the flowers that lie at his feet." We are always prone to take for granted that which is in front of our eyes, while giving a lot more importance to that which is away from us, in the past or in the future.

For example, what importance have you given to the great 1989 revolution that obliterated the Evil Empire of the Soviet Union? Do you see it as the momentous event that it is? Do you see that it is at least as important, if not more important, than the French Revolution of 1789 which itself was created by the Age of Reason? Do you see the hand of the Hierarchy behind this event of 1989? Do you recognize the externalization of the Hierarchy, as the Tibetan would say, in that event?

Do you experience in your life the ever-increasing presence of Christ? Have you given enough attention to the incredibly revolutionary dispensations that have been given to us in this century? Or do you choose to live in the past, worship that which is erroneously called the Scriptures, i.e., the Bible, and thus be part of the dead rather than be part of the living? You are missing the point.

You, too, are not seeing the living Christ and you are not recognizing Him. He is here in front of our eyes, manifesting to us all over the place, in every possible area of human endeavour. Instead, most people choose to look away from all of this, minimizing the importance of all of these momentous events of our time.

# NUMBER FIFTY-EIGHT

*His disciples said to him: "Is circumcision useful or not?" He said to them: "If it was useful, their father would beget them from their mother [already] circumcised. But [only] the true circumcision in the spirit gives all profit!"*

Have you ever been to a Jewish circumcision? If you have, you will have found it to be bloody, barbaric and primitive. In the first place, the argument of cleanliness in circumcision is fallacious. Common sense and hygiene would very easily take care of this issue. Besides, the issue of cleanliness could be argued about other parts of the body that accumulate dirt. Does that mean that we should eliminate those parts of the body as well in order to ensure cleanliness?

In the second place, circumcision is more an Egyptian than an Hebraic tradition. The Jews took their practice from the Egyptians. Not only did they take that practice from them, but they also took from them the fallacious argument of cleanliness. So, there is nothing vainglorious, revealed, or holy about this barbarism.

In the third place, this is a representation of symbolic castration—making the son submit to "the will of the father," as in cutting somebody's wings. This points to the need to curb rebelliousness.

Wouldn't it have been smarter, as the Christ suggests, instead of dealing with it by symbolically cutting part of the penis, to practice circumcision in the spirit, i.e., the purification process, dealing with and dissolving the salient, angular, aggressive aspects of the negativity of the lower self? As the Christ points out, if that is done, then all profit is reaped. All benefits, remember, are derived from the purification of the lower self.

In the fourth place, as modern science is demonstrating, the circumcised penis numbs itself a lot quicker than the uncircumcised one which has the nerves under much better protection. The result, of course, is less potency, less virility, less pleasure.

Aren't we looking at a primitive process of punishment by the withholding of pleasure? Aren't we looking at a reluctance to experience and a fear of pleasure supreme? That would be very much in accordance with the old and obsolete martinet teachings of the Jewish religion and much less in accordance with the laws of nature. As Christ Himself says, if God had wanted children circumcised, He would have done it.

# NUMBER FIFTY-NINE

*Jesus says: "Blessed are the poor, for the Kingdom of heaven is yours!"*

The poor here are those who leave their baggage behind. Rich people do not like to die because they cannot take their wealth with them and because they do not know whether they will be wealthy beyond the material world. The Byzantine Emperor Justinian, who was grossly self-indulgent and whose atrocities are comparable to those of Caligula and Nero, was responsible for the final withdrawal of any mention of reincarnation from Christian teachings. He saw to it that they were all wiped out because he was himself afraid of eternal life. He knew that at death he would have to face the consequences of his enormous misdeeds. He and his wife, the empress Theodora—who was a whore and who successfully seduced Justinian into marrying her—ferociously pursued and wiped out everything that mentioned the existence of life outside of the body. It is Christianity's great loss to have allowed such a low-life couple to dictate its beliefs for the ensuing fifteen hundred years and perhaps beyond. Maybe Christianity and the Catholic Church will come to their senses and realize this incredible blunder committed a millennium and a half ago. Who knows? There are no signs of this happening, however.

The poor here are the natural ones. Compare to Matthew 5:3, "Blessed are the poor in spirit, for theirs is the kingdom of heaven." Those who are poor in spirit do not have the intellectual baggage that prevents them from the simple and unaffected experience of the reality of God.

*A Commentary on the Gospel of Thomas*

In none of the professions which I have practiced have I had a formal education. I have a degree in mathematics. My success in business came without a business degree. My success as a psychotherapist in New York in the early 1980s came without a degree. The founding of The Church of the Path® and all of those spiritual teachings with which I work was done without formal education. "Credentials" can be, and in most cases are, an impediment to the experience of God.

Careful now! This does not mean that we have to keep ourselves in ignorance as did the Catholic Church in its misinterpretation of these sayings. All of the knowledge that I have acquired, which is considerable, has been done on my own, by myself.

"Blessed are the poor" means blessed are those who do not have any baggage in spirit or in the body. In the New Age we believe in abundance. This means that we can have baggage, but the baggage needs to be purified. If your possessions are put to good use, then you own them and they do not own you. They are no longer baggage; they have become part of the Kingdom of Heaven. It is when you are possessed by them, when you rely on them, depend on them, sell out and capitulate to them that the perversion exists. Then you have an anti-life situation in which the spirit is the slave to possessions, the lion eats the man.

# NUMBER SIXTY

*Jesus says: "He who does not hate his father and mother cannot be my disciple; and if he does not hate his brother and sister and does not take up his cross like me, he will not become worthy of me!"*

This is perhaps the most important saying of the Christ because it addresses specifically and directly the process of purifying the child within us. Although it is to be found in many places in the Scriptures, it has never been given its due, nor has its been recognized.

Matthew 10:37-38:
He that loveth father or mother more than me is not worthy of me: and he that loveth son or daughter more than me is not worthy of me. And he that taketh not his cross, and followeth after me, is not worthy of me.

Luke 14:26-27:
If any man come to me, and does not hate his father, and mother and wife, and children, and brethren, and sisters, yea, and his own life also, he cannot be my disciple. And whosoever doth not bear his cross, and come after me, cannot be my disciple.

Even New Age scriptures have not until now correctly interpreted what the Christ meant.

We at The Church of the Path® have ample material that proves that it is essential to get to the point where outrage is experienced towards one's physical family before entrance into the kingdom of God is possible. Not only must outrage be experienced at one's physical family, but one is also to feel outrage at conventional religion and at the process of being compelled to believe in a particular way, to act in a particular way, to say particular things when one does not believe them, to seek people's approval at the expense of one's own integrity. We have all been corrupted in this certain way. It goes as follows:

Before birth, the soul finds itself in a condition of at-onement with God. This means that all of its needs and wants are immediately, instantly met and satisfied, completely and totally. In the world of the infinite, there is no distance between cause and effect. In fact, cause and effect do not exist; they are one. The Law of Cause and Effect is unnecessary. Conversely, in spheres of development that are a lot lower than ours, the distance between cause and effect is so great and the connection between the two is so difficult that the pain of injustice—the greatest pain in human existence—is experienced continuously and perpetually. This is hell.

The greatest disappointment in a person's life comes at birth. The instant a person is born he experiences the fact that his needs are not met. The despair that ensues is immense, incredible. The magnitude of this despair leads the child to look upon one of his parents, or even perhaps on both, as being the source of fulfillment. Although this fulfillment cannot be as perfect as what he remembers, he understands that he has to make do with what is given to him. The parent, therefore, becomes God. All of the child's longing for at-onement with God becomes the child's longing for at-onement with that particular parent. The child, therefore, exhibits total and unconditional love toward this parent. He sells out to this parent completely.

The parent, on the other hand, who has embittered themself into believing that they would never again experience the goodness and total love of God, finds in the child's total and unconditional love for them a little God that they can control. This is as close as the parent ever feels in his life to finding total fulfillment. They now want to possess that little God and to form the child in their own image. So we have a double collusion:

1) The child, in his search for God, albeit misguided, sells out to the parent and allows the parent to mould and dictate his life. He conforms, believes, becomes whatever the parent wants him to become.

2) The parent, in his misguided search for God, deifies the child, possesses him, demands from him and at the same time sells out to him. This creates either a monster of rebellion and dictatorship—the child tyrant—or a monster of conformism, which if looked at closely, are really one and the same.

These unholy alliances are created by misperception of our parents. Indeed, we reduce our parents to robot-like proportions for our purposes, either to imitate them or denigrate them or both. The perception of who and what they really are will (a) free us of the negative contract and of the bondage to them and (b) restore in us our capacity to love them in the right way—the ultimate way—in the open, joyous, giving way that is not unhealthily dependent. At that point, our parents will no longer be our parents, they will be our friends, they will be our fellow Christians, they will be our fellow workers on the Path.

This unholy alliance continues in adulthood. The child will seek this mutual admiration society in all other life circumstances. Of course, great unhappiness will result. Furthermore, it will be impossible for the individual to gain a true perception of God. Therefore, it will be impossible for the individual to reach God unless and until this unholy pact is renounced and denounced. See our "Prayer to Renounce Substitutes for God[3]."

The reaching of this point—which we call the point of relinquishing—carries with it a genuine revolution in a person's life. Indeed, everything comes into question, not only the person's beliefs, but also his choice of career, his choice of mate, the construction of his persona, etc.

**It is only when a person has gone through this crisis and successfully overcome it that he becomes a true Christian, a follower, a disciple of the Christ.**

Taking up "his cross" refers to the crucifixion of the ego. After we have found our mother/father split (see my book, *Know Thyself*), the next step is to bring together the positive aspects of both sides of our duality and contrast them with our negative aspects. Then we are to take our negative aspects and find the positive components within them.

Gradually and experientially, as we bring all of this back to life, we have crucified the little ego that we had heretofore erected through the unholy alliance with our parents. To do this, our parents have to be given up. We also have to give up our sisters, our brothers, our children and everybody else.

This, of course, can be avoided if all of these good people are willing to do what we are doing—relinquish their parents, their siblings, their offspring and their unholy

---

[3] Found in *Prayers and Code of Conduct on the Path* by Reverend Dr. Albert Gani, page 48.

alliances. In this case, then, good work can start.

# NUMBER SIXTY-ONE

*Jesus says: "He who has known the world has fallen into a corpse; and he who has fallen into a corpse, the world is not worthy of him!"*

Knowing the world is being of the world, in other words, falling for the desire for approval of the world, for worldly goods, for position, for money, all pursued as if they were God Himself. These activities will make you fall into a corpse, into death, into that which is petrified and putrefied. In other words, you will deaden yourself; the deceleration of energy which we so often mention transforms you into a corpse.

You do all of this without really being aware of the fact that you have fallen into deadness. The minute that you become aware of the fact that you have fallen into deadness, you discover the corpse into which you have fallen. This discovery, this identification of deadness, of the lower self, will raise you above the world. The world out there will not be worthy of you anymore.

Here the Christ is describing a process—the process of falling into, becoming aware of, and finally relinquishing, the world and its glamours.

# NUMBER SIXTY-TWO

*Jesus says: "The Kingdom of the Father is like a man who has [good] seed [in his field.] By night his enemy came and sowed tares over the seed which is good. [But] this man did not allow them [his servants] to pluck up the tares, 'for fear', he told them, 'that in going to take away the tares, you carry off the wheat with it. But on the harvest day the tares will be recognisable; they will be taken away and burnt.'"*

This is very reminiscent of the parable in Matthew 13:24-30 explained by the Christ in Matthew 13:36-43. Our explanation, however, is somewhat different. The good seed in the field is the good people, or the good dispensation that is sent by the kingdom of God, by nature. Notice here, we do not limit ourselves to human beings when describing seed. We also include dispensation, positive or negative as it is.

The devil comes in by night and sows weeds (tares); By the word "devil" I mean a representative of the dark forces, the forces of deception, of untruth, of involution. When the servant asks the master whether the weeds should be plucked up, the master wisely answers no, explaining that if this were to be done too soon, the good seeds would be lost with the bad ones. Better it is to wait until they grow in order to differentiate between the tares and the wheat. It is very easy to recognize the good from the bad when we let the Law of Cause and Effect take its course, allowing understanding to occur and right judgment to be possible. Down the line, the difference will be very apparent. We can then identify the bad and dissolve it while enjoying the good. Otherwise, one runs the risk of throwing baby out with bath water. Nothing here is mentioned about Judgment Day. Nothing is as linear, as definitive or as punitive.

This very much applies to our code of conduct and the rules of confrontation. You may sense a character defect in somebody. However, you really have no right to confront him on it—unless he is on a Path of Purification alongside you, a path such as the one which we practice here at The Church of the Path®. You have no right to confront him unless the character defect has had a distinctive manifestation that can be pointed out and that has affected you or somebody else personally. Then, and only then, do you have the right to confront. If you confront before that, you run the risk of alienating this person totally, i.e., alienating not only that which is bad in him but also that which is good and possibly purposeful in your relationship to him.

# NUMBER SIXTY-THREE

*Jesus says: "Blessed is the man who has laboured; he has found Life!"*

It is interesting to note that in other translations of the Gospel of Thomas, the word "laboured" is seen to be synonymous to pain. Indeed, in our culture, labour is synonymous to pain. Something that is labourious means that it requires a lot of painstaking effort. A woman is in labour when she is in pain giving birth to a child. Creation is, therefore, forever condemned to be a painful process.

This need not be so. It is a freeze, a misconception. Labour is a blessed thing. Labour is movement. I much prefer the definition in physics in which labour is a function of movement of an object in time and space; there is no burden of pain attached to movement. In actuality, movement is a lot closer to pleasure than it is to pain. Movement becomes pain when it is resisted. Without resistance, movement is pleasure. One moves towards pleasure and away from pain. So, labour is blessed. Labour is life. Find labour and you will be blessed and you will have found life. Find your task, the labour of your life, and you will be blessed and you will have found the reason for your life.

# NUMBER SIXTY-FOUR

*Jesus says: "Seek to see Him who is living, while you are living; rather than to die and to seek to see Him [only] when you can no longer see Him!"*

*Just then a Samaritan was going into Judea carrying a lamb. He [=Jesus] said to His disciples: "What [will] this man [do] with the lamb?" They answered: "He will kill it and eat it!" But he said to them: "He will not eat it as long as it is still alive, but only if he kills it and it becomes a corpse." They said to him: "In no other way will he hurt it!" [Then] he said to them: "You yourselves, then, seek a place of rest so that you do not become corpses and are eaten!"*

This is referred to in several places in Luke and John. It is an exhortation by the Christ for His disciples to recognize Him as their Master and to take full advantage of His presence by seeking to see His reality. He is asking them to see Him here and now rather than to wait for death. It is not given that at death they will find the Christ. He is trying to tell them how fortunate they are to have Him present in flesh and blood, that the proximity and the availability of these teachings will not last forever and cannot be found in death.

It is the Christ's intent to have His disciples accelerate their process by realizing the unique opportunity presented to them by His presence, "while you are living."

Beyond this obvious explanation exists another one. "While you are living," is when you are aware. The greater your awareness the more alive you are; you can then seek to see Him and you will find Him. When you lose that awareness, you are dead and you are not able to find Him. We all have periods of awareness during which we can seek the presence of God and find it much more readily than at other times when the presence of God cannot be felt. The presence of God is permanent and continuous. Our state of aliveness and of awareness is not.

The second part of Number Sixty-Four should be a totally separate entry, as it is in other translations. If we make the connection between being alive and being aware, the meaning of this parable will become very clear. Indeed, being aware protects you from being slaughtered and eaten, i.e., protects you from being taken advantage of, from being cannibalized, and from having your essence stolen from you. It is reminiscent of Number Forty, the saying about the robber who is able to enter a person's house if that person has his hands tied. If they are not tied, the owner can defend his house. Having your full faculties awake is the best possible protection you can have. If you are alive (aware), you are safe even if you are a lamb (innocent).

The place of rest to be sought, again, is a place of awareness. Awareness, aliveness is also peace, inner peace, balance, the state of balance. Inner peace is the state of being able to sustain tension. In philosophy we find the same concept in synthesis being the unifying state arrived at through the experience of thesis and antithesis.

# NUMBER SIXTY-FIVE

*Jesus says: "Two will lie down there on one bed: one will die, the other will live."*

*Salome says: "Who art thou, man; from whom hast thou [come forth,] that thou shouldst lie on my couch and eat at my table?" Jesus says to her: "I am he who has been brought into being by Him who is equal [to me:] I have been given what belongs to my Father!"—"I am thy disciple!"*

*Because of that, I say this: When [a person] finds himself solitary, he will be full of light; but when he finds himself divided, he will be full of darkness.*

When Salome says to the Christ, "Who are you, man, to lie on my couch?" doesn't that sound like they have just had sex or that they are about to have sex? It does to me. Lying on a woman's couch and eating at her table are what we have all done with our girlfriends. It also sounds as if the Christ has actively, almost aggressively, decided that He was going to have sex with Salome since she says, Who are you to just come in and do this? Furthermore, albeit not as blatantly, the first line also sounds like a sexual engagement.

However, look at what the prudes did to it: Luke 17:34-35: "I tell you, in that night there will be two men in one bed; the one will be taken and the other left. There will be two women grinding together; one will be taken and the other left." In his attempt to desexualize—castrate—the original event, Luke here makes us think that perhaps he advocates homosexuality. I do not think he does it intentionally, but from his misguided view of sexuality, it certainly sounds as if that is what he is saying.

Matthew 24:40-41 is a little more discreet: "Then two men will be in the field; one is taken and one is left. Two women will be grinding at the mill; one is taken and one is left." No matter which translation you take of the Gospel of Thomas and no matter which papyrus you consider, you still have Christ climbing on Salome's couch and eating from her table in a presumptuous manner. Editing this passage of its sexual content, reducing it and misinterpreting it is a blatant act of emasculation of the Christ. As far as I am concerned, Christ here demonstrates that He is a very actively sexual person.

What is wrong with that? Wasn't He supposed to enter into three-dimensional reality and go through the normal life of a human being? Isn't sexuality part of the normal life of the human being? By having sex, doesn't He demonstrate that sexuality is a very nice thing to do?

Why is one dying and the other one living? Because sexuality, as in anything else in life, is dependent upon intent. Two people can go to bed with one another, one with a negative intent and the other with a positive intent. The one with the negative intent commits a sin, the one with a positive intent is undergoing a wonderful experience. Death is the obvious consequence of negative intent. A person who is using or abusing another on the sexual level is decelerating his energy and encountering death. However, the other person who is honestly and with goodwill undergoing a sexual experience will be enlivened by it.

When Salome asks Christ who He is to want to have sex with her and to want to share her table, He responds that He is the Son of God and in that essence He is equal to Him. Therefore, God has sexual feelings! Of course He does. And why not? Sexuality is the essence of the universe. It is the secret of creativity. Any creation involves a masculine principle penetrating a feminine principle.

As to the last portion of that saying, we must understand the word "solitary" as meaning "unified." A solitary person is someone who has found unity within himself. Someone is solitary to the degree he has been able to unify his conflicts. To that extent, then, he will be full of light. But, divided and in conflict, he is full of darkness.

This then also points to the necessity for each one of us to find within ourselves our animus or our anima. Men are to find their female part within themselves, women are to find their male part within themselves. This is what it means to be in one bed. This is the purpose of sexuality. The process of unification can only happen when we come together with that aspect in us which has the opposite gender. Unlike many teachings—including some New Age ones—this process will not happen through emasculation, through androgyny or through denying one's sex. This process will happen through the total and full experience of sexuality which is nothing else but the most explicit manifestation of love that can be found in the human experience.

Isn't it strange to see Christ as an asexual person? Why should He, the personification of love, not have experienced sexuality, the most beautiful expression of it?

# NUMBER SIXTY-SIX

*Jesus says: "When I tell my mysteries to [...] mystery: [what] your right hand does, let your left hand not know [that] it does it."*

This incomplete saying is urging us not to divulge spiritual teachings to those who are not ready to receive them. It points to the dual life of the disciple who has to be capable of speaking a common language with everybody and at the same time interacting and transacting on a much higher level with his fellow disciples. It reminds us of Christ's comfort in the company of criminals and discomfort in the company of Pharisees. He could speak the language of the criminals since they were honest about who they were as opposed to the Pharisees who were unreachable through their many layers of masks, pretenses, and self-idealizations.

It reminds me of my own friendship with a tennis player who had neither the desire nor the inclination to be spiritual. Nevertheless, I enjoyed his company, and I later discovered, much to my surprise, that I had been his best friend. However, I could not talk to him about the "mysteries" that we study and follow on the Path. On his particular level, he was reachable and he was honest. He had no pretenses concerning who he was. For example, he had no compunctions or problems about betraying people with whom he had commitments. And he had no hesitancy talking to me about it. He did not talk to them about it because he was a liar and a thief of feelings. However, I could reach him. He was a "criminal" in an admitted manner in his interaction with me.

By contrast there were others who were Pharisees. They pretended not to be sinners. They also pretended to believe in the mysteries—to believe in God, to believe in Christ, to be good church goers—while at the same time carrying on hypocritically behind everybody's back. Those I could neither reach nor befriend.

# NUMBER SIXTY-SEVEN

*Jesus says: "There was a rich man who had many possessions. He said [to himself:] 'I will use my wealth to sow my field, to plant, to fill my barn with harvest, so that need will not touch me.' Such were the things that he thought in his heart. But during the night, he died. He who has ears to hear, let him hear!"*

This is the story of so many of us who are trying to avoid feeling any need. We attempt to satisfy ourselves by accumulating wealth, thinking it will provide safety and security. We do this not only on the physical level but also on the emotional and on the mental levels. We would rather compromise our integrity than experience need.

However, without need there is no fulfillment. Only he who needs finds fulfillment and finds the truth. One has to look for the truth in order to find it. And, therefore, one has to feel a need for it. Feeling a need for something involves experiencing the possibility of not having it, of never having it. The person who is able to experience need without demanding immediate gratification has found the secret of life. Most of us exaggerate our needs, believing that the more exaggerated they are, the more likely we are to have them satisfied immediately. We then sink into despair which is the other side of demand. All is for naught, and we die, never having enjoyed the moment or anything that we actually possess.

The capacity to experience one's need eventually brings one in touch with one's instincts, which is nothing else than the Universal Life Force. It is through reconnection with instincts that everything becomes possible.

The Instinct of Self-Preservation will lead to immortality; the Instinct of Procreation will lead, strangely enough, to God, to religion, through at-onement with another person; the Herd Instinct will bring you to civilization; the Self-Assertion Instinct will bring you to self-actualization; and finally, the Instinct of Enquiry, the highest and the most sophisticated instinct, will bring you to the state of knowing, which is the highest possible state that you can attain.

Death comes to him who does not need because he has taken himself away from instincts through overprotection. This is what happened to this man who died during the night.

# NUMBER SIXTY-EIGHT

*Jesus says: "A man had guests. When he had prepared the feast, he sent his servant to call these guests. He went to the first and said to him: 'My master invites thee!' [The other] replied: 'I am due to receive some money from some merchants; they are coming to see me this evening and I am going to give them orders. I ask to be excused from the feast.' [The servant] went to another and said to him: 'My master has invited thee.' [He] said to him: 'I have bought a house and I am needed for the day: I am not free.' He went to another and said to him: 'My master invites thee!' [He] replied: 'My friend is being married and I am giving a feast [for him]. I will not come; I ask to be excused from the feast!' He went to another and said to him: 'My master invites thee!' [He] said to him: 'I have bought a field (?) and I have not yet been to receive the revenue [from it]. I will not be coming; I ask to be excused from the feast!' The servant returned and said to his master: 'Those whom you invited to the feast have excused themselves.' The master said to his servant: 'Go out into the streets and those whom you find, bring in to dine.' The buyers and mer[chants will not enter] into the places of my Father.'"*

This reminds me of all of the people we invite to our workshops, to our meditations, and to our services. We are inviting them to a feast, an abundance of spiritual food. What we mostly get as responses have to do with these people's involvement with their materialism, with that which they are bonded to or with that of which they are afraid, just as in this saying. Look at the reasons why these people do

not respond to the master's invitation:
- receiving some money.
- buying a house.
- going to a friend's wedding.
- collecting revenue from a field.

We can add more to these:
- going to a church that is more acceptable.
- being seen in a climate and atmosphere of respectability.
- being too fearful to be discovered for the cowards or the liars that they really are.
- being suddenly overcome by a minor affliction.

These excuses show that these people are too busy finding fulfillment through seeking approval or through cultivating materialism. The master finally resorts to inviting anyone who wants to come. He goes in the streets and collects those people who want to come to the feast, those people who are not tied to all of these "obligations" which are, in the last analysis, unimportant.

And notice the last sentence "the buyers and merchants will not enter into the places of my Father." Doesn't that remind you of the eye of the needle of Matthew 19? Indeed, the Christ said, "It is easier for a camel to go through the eye of a needle than for a rich man to enter the Kingdom of Heaven." The buyers and merchants are the rich people who will not enter into the places of God. On the contrary, those people who were invited off the street, who in those days were obviously the poor and the beggars, have a much greater chance to make it to the kingdom of God.

# NUMBER SIXTY-NINE

*He said: "An [important] man had a vineyard which he gave to cultivators so that they should work it and he should receive the fruit from them. He sent his servant so that the cultivators should give him the fruit of the vineyard: [but] they seized his servant, beat him and almost killed him. The servant came back and told this to his master. His master said [to himself] 'Perhaps he did not recognize them?' He sent another servant: the cultivators beat this one also. Then the master sent his son: he said to himself: 'No doubt they will respect my child?' But when they realized that this was the heir to the vineyard, these cultivators seized him and killed him. He who has ears let him hear!"*

Here the Christ is essentially predicting His death. The servants sent by the master to the cultivators are the prophets sent by God to educate humanity. The cultivators, i.e., humanity, are merely borrowing the land on which they are working. It is not their land; it is God's land. We are merely borrowing this nature, this Earth, this universe. We are working on it and are on probation, being tested in God's vineyard.

God—the Master—sends His Son, hoping that they will at least recognize and respect Him since they have not respected the servants who were unceremoniously beaten up and thrown out. They killed the Son because they realized that He was the heir to the vineyard. In other words, He was going to claim the vineyard back to the Master. Indeed, this is what Christ did. He entered the temple at Jerusalem and tried to return it to what it was supposed to be, the house of God. For that, He was killed.

Each person's task resembles this process. When you discover your task, you will find out how your duty is to revolutionize that which heretofore you have done. If you dare bring about the revolution, which actually consists of your task, you will be hated, you will be rejected, you will be despised, and you might even be killed, depending upon how revolutionary is your task. Nevertheless, the Master still owns the vineyard and is in the process of claiming it back. So watch out!

The master "should receive the fruit" from the cultivators. In the last analysis, all of our possessions are God's. We are merely users of our possessions. We do not really own anything. We temporarily control things which are actually borrowed by us who come in and go away. The ownership rests with God, the Eternal.

# NUMBER SEVENTY

*Jesus says: "Would that thou couldst tell me about the stone which the builders have rejected! It is that one, the cornerstone."*

Nothing is to be rejected. That which is rejected becomes the most important element. They rejected Him who was the most important human being who ever walked the Earth. In science, we have to wait until the eighteenth century to have someone enunciate the same principle. Indeed, Lavoisier, the French scientist and chemist of the eighteenth century, is known to have said, "Nothing is lost and nothing is found." Every single atom in the universe can be accounted for and can be explained in its existence and in its purpose. Nothing can or should be disregarded.

Is this the way you conduct your life? To what extent do you disregard things, let them slip you by? And how then do they become the focal point of your life, perhaps in a negative way? It is, therefore, those negativities which *have* to be dealt with that, in the last analysis, will yield to you the possibility of finally being a total human being. Think of your unconscious, for instance, as being the repository of that which you have discarded, disregarded. It is that, but it is also the cornerstone of your life. All of your strength, all of that which determines the course of your life is unconscious. The conscious part of you, the ego function, merely navigates, acts as a rudder to the forces that are to be found in the unconscious.

# NUMBER SEVENTY-ONE

*Jesus says: "He who knows the All, but has failed to know himself, has failed completely to know, [or: to find] the Place!"*

Here is another exhortation from the Christ to know yourself. Any knowledge that is not backed up by self-knowledge is worthless. Any knowledge that does not correspond to an experiential knowledge within one's self is equally worthless. All learning serves only one purpose: the purpose of finding the Place, which is none other than the Higher Self, God. This Higher Self can only be found through self-knowledge, therefore, from within. It cannot be found outside of the self. So, the Socratic exhortation, "Know thyself," is key to all spirituality and to all religion.

This is exactly what we practice at The Church of the Path®. This is what the new dispensation is all about in the New Age. This is why we have called the book that contains the fundamental material of the Path, *Know Thyself*.

Once again, if we are to think about mundane psychotherapy, or psychology or psychiatry from this point of view, we can see its ultimate fallacy. It is not through outer knowledge acquired in universities that a person becomes a counselor, a healer of the soul ("psyche" in Greek), a psychotherapist. It is only through deep identification and experiential inner knowledge that the counselor can help anyone at all. The counselor must be able to deeply experience anything that the counselee is going through. This capacity to empathize with any and all human experience is the whole point of Christ's incarnating on this

Earth and serving as an example. He came to familiarize Himself with every single aspect of human existence, especially the evil and negativity of it. So should the counselor be such a person who, knowing himself thoroughly, is thus able to help others.

# NUMBER SEVENTY-TWO

*Jesus says: "Blessed are you when you are hated and persecuted; but they will not find a position in that place to which they shall pursue you!"*

The Christ here is addressing the necessary process that any innovator must go through—being hated and persecuted. Understanding that each individual's task is one of innovation and uniqueness, you will realize (a) how very few people there are who have discovered their task and are actually bringing it into manifestation, and (b) why so many others resist it.

One must go through the long dark tunnel of instability and reach the Higher Self in order to find one's task. Only then can the task be accomplished. Once found, the task manifests in a world in which there exists compromise and negative stability. This task then disrupts the pseudo-stability, challenges and exposes the dishonesty and compromise, and brings innovation. The process always starts in the immediate vicinity of the person whose task is being accomplished. Thus, the person is outrightly rejected by his immediate environment. The task then takes root in environments that are different from the original one in which the innovator lived.

The persecutors have never made it through the long dark tunnel. They live in negative security. They are afraid of and are threatened by the long dark tunnel. They, therefore, drive away from their realm the innovator, the liberator, the avatar, who goes into the realm of the Higher Self, the realm of God "in which they will not find a position."

*A Commentary on the Gospel of Thomas*

# NUMBER SEVENTY-THREE

*Jesus says: "Blessed are those who are persecuted in their hearts. They are those who have known (?) the Father in truth! Blessed are those who are hungry, because they will satisfy their bellies to [their] content!"*

The persecution theme is taken up again here. Now we are dealing with the heart. Being persecuted in your heart means that your love is rejected. This problem can also exist on a more subtle level. Someone may have a capacity to give and may find himself frustrated—there is no one to receive it, no one to understand the nature or the depth of what he has to give. This is to be found usually in people of genius in any field of endeavour. The Christ must have felt that to an enormous extent, perhaps more than anybody else.

If you have opened your heart, you have "known the Father in truth." Having done so, you are bringing back this truth to those who are in distortion, threatening their distortion which is about the only thing they have to hold on to. That is why they persecute you.

The hunger that is being referred to here is the need. The ability to need and to express one's need without maximizing it, minimizing it, numbing it or agonizing over it corresponds to one's ability to love. He who knows how to need knows how to love. That is why he who knows how to need will be satisfied, whether in material goods such as food or in the substance of the heart (which is feelings) or love.

# NUMBER SEVENTY-FOUR

*Jesus says: "When you have something left to share among you, what you possess will save you. But if you cannot share [among you], that which you have not among you, that [...?... will...] you.*

The second sentence should read as follows: "But if you cannot share among you that which you have not among you, that which you have not will kill you."

First of all the Christ, points out that you have to share what you have. Everyone has something to share. No one is so poor so as not to have anything to share. The act of sharing whatever it is you have saves you.

This is not an altruistic, goody two-shoes saying. This is the Spiritual Law of Abundance: share what you have and abundance will come to you.

It makes excellent business sense. People do not succeed in business by hoarding their goods and not sharing them with the universe. It is by making your wealth work for you, i.e., by sharing it with everybody else, that you maximize its potentials and, therefore, make it grow. Spiritual Law always makes very good business sense. The key to abundance is through loving, caring and giving.

However, not only does it make business sense, but it also makes spiritual sense. If you share what you have, you will be saved. The key to salvation is through sharing and giving, through the total participation of the universe with your brothers and sisters in humanity.

So squander yourself on the universe, explode and let the particles of you become food for your brothers and sisters in the world. Stop hoarding, stop conserving. Stop pickling yourself. What are you saving for? Who is going to enjoy you when you are all embittered and shriveled up? How much are you enjoying yourself as you are hoarding? How are you being a slave to your own possessions rather than having your possessions be moulded by you, be used by you, and live out their task?

However, if you cannot share—which is impossible, i.e., if you **will not** share—that which you have, then "that which you do not have will kill you." That which you do not have, this lack, is an impossibility. Just as evil is an impossibility. It is a lie. Saying, "I do not have anything to share" is always a lie. Therefore, it will kill you, because it will disconnect you from others. You will find yourself isolated through not giving. The little which you already have will be continually diminished until it disappears completely, and until it loses you as well. You will find yourself not only being stingy with what you have in material goods, but also stingy with your feelings, with your thoughts and with your actions. You will then stop living, since life is movement, participation, communication, relationship, giving and taking.

# NUMBER SEVENTY-FIVE

*Jesus says: "I will [...] and no one will be able [....]*

Compare with Matthew 26:61: "and said, 'This fellow said, "I am able to destroy the temple of God, and to build it in three days."'"

Compare with Matthew 27:40: "and saying, 'You who would destroy the temple and build it in three days, save yourself! If you are the Son of God, come down from the cross.'"

Mark 14:58: "We heard him say, 'I will destroy this temple that is made with hands, and in three days I will build another, not made with hands.'"

Mark 15:29: "And those who passed by derided him, wagging their heads, and saying, 'Aha! You who would destroy the temple and build it in three days.'"

John 2:19: "Jesus answered them, 'Destroy this temple, and in three days I will raise it up.'"

This is a very powerful saying and I would not be surprised if, in this particular papyrus, someone had deliberately excised the words that he found disturbing so as to make the saying more palatable. Indeed, as seen in the Bible Gospels, the Christ was later berated for having said these words at the temple on Tuesday of Holy Week.

In order to understand this saying, we have to tell the story of the task of Christ as revealed to us twentieth century esoteric teachers. The point of Christ's incarnation was not to bring new teachings. His teachings parallel those already imparted by other great teachers. His task was to earn the right to do battle with the devil after His death as a human being. As soon as He died, He summoned the Forces of Light which were ready to follow Him in battle. For three days He battled the devil and frayed a passage for us to make it to the kingdom of God. The three days of that battle constitute His building of the temple anew.

It is not merely, as John suggests, that He referred to His being resurrected in three days, i.e., resurrecting His body—His private temple—to life. That He did, too. However, He was also referring to the building of a real temple, the Temple of God. His exhortation to the Jews to destroy their present corrupt temple was done so as to enable Him to build a new temple in three days. Had they destroyed their old ways and the old temple, the battle against the forces of darkness would have begun right then and there, and the kingdom of God would have been established on Earth without waiting for it to be established through the passage frayed on the astral level.

The degree to which you agree to swiftly—and without hesitation—destroy your old ways and the negativities that go with them is commensurate to the degree to which you will then build a new life. You can only be reborn if you die. The death that needs to occur is the death of all that you have heretofore burdened yourself with, all of the falsehoods, the negativities, the compromises, the sellouts, etc.

# NUMBER SEVENTY-SIX

*[Someone (?) said] to him: "Speak to my brothers, that they may share with me my father's possessions!" He answered him: "Man, who made me a sharer?" He turned to his disciples and said to them: "Let me not be a sharer!"*

Here we have yuppiedom two thousand years ago. This is an attempt by somebody to use spirituality for materialism. He wants the Christ to convince his brothers to share their inheritance with him, "my father's possessions." In His response, the Christ gives two answers:

1) Inheritance does not make sense. You find your value within yourself. The only valid inheritance is what God gives you. In our community we have seen positive proof of the destructive aspects of inheritance. Inheritance debilitates. It takes people away from, not towards, the realization of their strength, their task, and their power.

2) "Let me not be a sharer" really means that He is not willing to compromise. Sharing is compromising. The Christ and His teachings are not about compromise. They are about the Absolute. One should not be interested in the scraps of an inheritance. One should be interested in finding and manifesting totality, the infinity of God's abundance.

Let's distinguish between the principle of sharing which characterizes the Law of Brotherhood and which, therefore, is one of the fundamental teachings of the Christ, and, on the other hand, sharing in the way it is meant in the context of this saying.

In this saying, the man wants the Christ to collude with

him in a greedy process of obtaining inheritance. This has nothing to do with sharing. It has to do with greed; it has to do with getting a certain amount of money or possessions without earning them.

True sharing can only occur when one has earned what it is that is being shared. Compare, for instance, this type of sharing to the very well known story of Saint Martin, sharing his coat with a beggar when it was very cold outside.

# NUMBER SEVENTY-SEVEN

*Jesus says: "The harvest is great but the labourers are few. Pray the Lord to send labourers for the harvest."*

The labourers referred to here are none other than the workers on the Path. We know so well how there are very few workers on the Path. Yet the harvest is great. The work to be done is huge. The worlds of pseudo-life, of compromise, of half-truths which are worse than lies, of inertia and materialism, of conceit and of self-will represent the fields that need to be harvested. We need many more labourers! We join Christ and His disciples in His prayer to send more labourers to join us in the painstaking work of the harvest.

It is a harvest. Those who labour in it benefit from it. The benefits are infinite. This reminds me of something that Tom Peters, the very successful business consultant and motivator, said when urging business people to serve the public, to give to the public, to be kind to their clients, rather than to take advantage of them. He said that if you do so you would have no competition because you would be the only one in your field doing so. After two thousand years of Christianity, it still remains true; those who live the ethical life, those who participate in the labour of the harvest, those people who are on a Path of Purification such as this one, are very few and far between indeed.

# NUMBER SEVENTY-EIGHT

*He said: "Lord, many are round the opening but nobody in the well!"*

This is really of the same theme as the preceding saying. Those who are around the opening of the well want to take advantage of the labour of those who have actually taken the trouble to go in the well and get the water.

At the end of World War II, in 1945, when the Allied victory was a certainty, a multitude of countries which had heretofore remained neutral suddenly declared war on the Axis Powers. I know this very well since I, at the time, was three years old and in Egypt. King Farouk of Egypt, who in his hypocrisy decided to remain neutral throughout the war in spite of the fact that the first Allied victory, El Alamein, happened to have been fought in his kingdom, declared war on Germany in 1945.

The Tibetan admonishes the pacifists in his message of June 30, 1940:

"I would say to those who preach a passive attitude in the face of evil and human suffering and who endorse a pacifism which involves no risks: With what do you propose to fight the forces of aggression, of treachery, evil and destruction which are today stalking over our planet? What weapons do you bring to this combat? How will you begin to stem the onslaught and arrest the whirlwind? Will you use prayers for peace, and then patiently wait for the forces of good to fight your battle and for God to do the work? I tell you that your prayers and your wishes are unavailing when divorced from right and potent action."[4]

We urge the Reader to read the entire message and be inspired by it accordingly.

Going into the well is a symbol of going into the tunnel, the long, dark tunnel at the end of which is the light or the water of life. Nobody can do it for you; you have to do it by yourself. You can be guided into it, however. And this is what the Christ and what the helpers on the Path do for you.

This is an opportunity for us to denounce pacifism as a euphemism for cowardice. As the Tibetan says, form destroyed in battle can easily be replaced by the process of reincarnation; however, the death of an idea or the subjugation of a people or the repression of spirituality are infinitely more damaging.

Past a certain point violence is indeed the only language that evil understands. Therefore, it is often right and necessary to effect military intervention, whether as a nation or as a community of nations.

Also, when one must resort to violence in order to redress the good. It is always because there has been procrastination, rationalization, the propagating and the toleration of half-truths—in other words, a lack of backbone and commitment to good—which permitted the evil to grow and solidify its position. This is abundantly demonstrated by history. Had Hitler been confronted early in his march across Europe, he would have collapsed very quickly, for example.

Do your work, fight your battles, jump in the well and draw your own water.

---

[4] Bailey, Alice A. *Externalization of the Hierarchy.* Lucis Publishing Company, New York, N.Y., 1957, pp. 232f.

# NUMBER SEVENTY-NINE

*Jesus says: "Many stand outside at the door, but it is only the solitaries who will enter into the bridal chamber."*

This theme is reminiscent of "many are called but few are chosen." Here, it is put in a volitional context. "Many stand outside at the door" because they do not wish to enter. They do not want to draw water themselves, they do not want to participate in the labours of the harvest, so they stand outside the door.

There is an incredible number of people who are ready to do this work on the Path but choose not to. They are open to the teachings of the Path, however, standing at the door, they do not actually enter. They do not commit themselves. They choose to remain butterflies, fluttering from one discipline to another, taking the goodies from one teacher here and another there, applying it to themselves as they please and whenever they please, while avoiding the penetration of the deep problems in their lives, rationalizing them, blaming the outside world for them, or pretending they simply do not exist.

It is a terrible loss! If all of these butterflies finally congregated—pardon the pun—we would have a huge force for the construction of the temple in three days (Matthew 26:61)[5], here in this three-dimensional reality, here on Earth.

So, they stand outside the door. In order to enter, one has to become at-one with oneself. This, again, is an explanation of the word "solitary." He who has resolved his

---

[5] See Commentary Number Seventy-Five.

dualities becomes solitary and is then able to enter. Enter what? Enter the bridal chamber! Here again is a reference to the sanctity of sexuality. He could have said "enter the door of initiation." He could have said "enter the door to the kingdom of God." But He did not; He said "the bridal chamber" which connotes—indubitably—sexuality, sexuality in a committed way, sexuality in the way that we understand it here on the Path.

He who has found unity within, or he who pursues unity within is ready for marriage with another human being. He is ready for union, for sexuality, for the bliss of at-onement on all levels with another person. Then he will experience the presence of God. It is in the bridal chamber that God resides for us. God will be found in sexual union, not outside it.

# NUMBER EIGHTY

*Jesus says: "The Kingdom of the Father is like a man, a merchant, who has a burden and found a pearl. This merchant is a wise man: he sold the bundle and bought the pearl alone. You also seek his treasure which does not perish, which lasts, into which the moth does not enter to consume and [where] the worm does not destroy."*

The merchant who has a burden is reminiscent of all of these people today who are burdened by their pursuit of money. You will find them mostly in the world of business, commerce and industry. In that sense, it is no different today than it was at the time of Christ, and that is why He chose to talk about a merchant with a burden.

The burden of the merchant, your burden, my burden, constitutes the possessions to which we attach ourselves. On the astral level, the burden is the way we enslave others in order to have them love us, or the way we let ourselves be enslaved by others in order to be loved. The burden constitutes the false life which we are so very much afraid to give up. Are you ready to give up your fears, your anxieties, for example? To what extent do you hold them dear, to what extent to you believe that it is the existence of your fears that makes you safe? This is one example of your burdens. The other two major examples are your conceit (that which you want to believe you are instead of that which you really are) and your self-will (your stubbornness, your demands which are known to bring you nothing but despair).

All of this is worthless when compared to the pearl of

wisdom to be found in your Higher Self. This pearl, as infinitesimally small as it appears to be from the angle of the physical, is infinitely great from the angle of the spiritual. In order to possess this pearl, you have to let go of the bundle. The price of this pearl is the bundle, is the burden. Possession of this pearl can only occur to the degree that you have given up your bundle. Real life is not available to you unless you have given up the false life.

Possession of this pearl will make you forever rich, forever safe. It cannot be taken away from you. It will last infinitely, it can be destroyed by neither moth nor by worm. The pearl—your Higher Self, at-onement with God, the state of being a "solitary"—is immune to evil. It cannot be attacked.

The pearl seems to have been found accidentally. Contact with the Higher Self first occurs accidentally. It is available when you least expect it. The process of finding the pearl and keeping it permanently is the process of voluntarily disengaging from your baggage. To the degree that you still hold on to baggage, to that degree you will not be able to have the pearl. Once you have found the pearl, you will not rest until you give up your baggage and possess the pearl once and for all.

The process of desiring the pearl and pursuing the pearl deliberately is the purification process we practice. It is, therefore, the process of disengaging from the baggage.

# NUMBER EIGHTY-ONE

*Jesus says: "I am the light which is on them all. I am the All, and the All has gone out from me and the All has come back to me. Cleave the wood: I am there; lift the stone and thou shalt find me there!"*

Here the Christ says several things:

1) He is stating that the light is personalized. God is an entity as is every human being. This is what is meant when He says "I am the All." However, it is not to be understood as a claim of exclusivity or a declaration of personality cultism. He is inviting everybody to be the All. Becoming the All is available to everybody, not just to Him. He happens to be in the position of imparting the knowledge that was given to Him by the All, and therefore, at that particular moment He represents the All, He is the All. So is a teacher to his students. So are parents to their children.

2) Christ also describes the process that occurred to Him through incarnation in our realm. In order to come into our realm, He had to relinquish all. "All has gone out from me." Imagine how painful it must have been for a being of His magnitude to lose contact with the Universal Life Force. Imagine how difficult it was for Him to encounter injustice, He who is justice, fairness, loving and giving. Imagine how desperate He must have been at the end of His life when He was forsaken by everybody, including, so He thought, God.

3) But "All has come back to me." Through the process of incarnation into three-dimensional reality, He rediscovers

All—God, the Universal Life Force, the Higher Self—and therefore,

4) Christ can be found everywhere, within the wood, under every stone, i.e., even material reality is alive and is potentially the All. The Christ exists in every atom of creation. Every atom of creation potentially is the Christ. You will find the Christ anywhere you look.

This saying demonstrates the degree to which Christianity was meant to embrace both immanence—finding God in the stone and in wood and in every human being—and transcendence—I am the All, I am the personalized God. In this saying the Christ beautifully brings together immanence and transcendence. Immanence was unfortunately taken away from Christianity to an extraordinary extent in the later misinterpretations of it. The transcendence that was left was a caricature of what it was in the beginning in Christ's teachings. Indeed, transcendence, when not separated from immanence, ceases to be a fanatical personality cult and acquires much more balanced proportions. God is a being with consciousness the way you are and I am and also is in every single atom of creation.

# NUMBER EIGHTY-TWO

Jesus says: *"Why did you go out into the country-side? [Was it] to see a reed shaken [by] the wind, and to see a m[an with soft] garments clothing him? [But they are in the dwelling-places of] kings and your great ones, those whom [soft garments] clothe, and they do not know the truth!"*

This corresponds to Matthew 11:7-8 and to Luke 7:24-25. This is what Christ seems to have said after having met with two disciples of John the Baptist. John the Baptist was in jail. He sent two messengers to question the Christ, apparently to make sure that He was the Messiah or that He was a prophet. After assuring the visitors as to His identity (which seems to have been done in Number Eighty-One), He turns to the crowd and tells them the saying of Number Eighty-Two.

Paraphrasing what He said: "What did you come here for? Did you come to see a weakling, one without backbone, one without integrity [a reed shaken by the wind]? Did you come to see a man with soft garments clothing him?", i.e., a man of means, a well-adjusted yuppie, a well-dressed preacher, as in the flashy TV evangelists with their fancy clothes and their well-made-up hair. They are buffoons to me as people with soft garments were at that time to the Christ.

Then He tells the crowd that if it is yuppies they are looking for, they came to the wrong place. These people—kings and the great ones, or the ones invested with authority—are all to be found in the same place. Not only was He talking about those having temporal power, but those holding spiritual and moral power. In our day, the pageantry of the Catholic Church with its extraordinarily complicated traditions (literally Byzantine), its outfits—the value of which are immeasurable in terms of money—of course, is a good example.

The Christ concludes that none of these people know the truth. We may as well conclude the same thing today. As always, the truth is not to be found in any of these conceited clubs. It is interesting to note that "and they do not know the truth" is conspicuously absent from Matthew and from Luke.

I am reminded here of an episode in Arab history. In the middle of the seventh century, the second Caliph after the Prophet Mohammed, Omar, entered into negotiations with the Byzantine emperor. The emperor sent his emissary who arrived sumptuously clothed in a litter, carried by equally sumptuously clothed slaves. Upon arrival at the Arab camp, the emperor's emissary inquired as to the whereabouts of Omar. He was told by a simple soldier, Omar? Do you see that guy over there sleeping on the sand and using his shoes as a pillow? That's Omar.

The destruction of a civilization seems to be commensurate to how sophisticated and elaborate become their leaders.

# NUMBER EIGHTY-THREE

*In the crowd a woman says to him: "Blessed is the womb which bore thee and the breast which fed thee!" He said to her: "Blessed are those who have heard the word of the Father and keep it! In truth, days are coming when you will say: Happy is the womb that has not brought forth and those breasts which have not given suck!"*

Obviously, the woman in the crowd is blessing Him by blessing His mother. This is very common in the Middle East. Whether you bless or curse somebody, you always refer to his mother. The Christ responds by saying that those who heard, understood and heeded the word of the Father are blessed, not through their mothers. The Christ makes it clear that it is independent of parents that we find blessing, proximity to God. The blessed are those people have heard the word of the Father and have kept it, i.e., have applied it.

It is tempting to interpret the second part of this saying in a way that is anti-sex. I have another interpretation. Twentieth century esoteric teachers warned people who wanted to become parents, telling them that the children who will be born in our era would come in with extraordinary amounts of energy and be very difficult to manage.

From the look of things, they were right on. Consider the incredible percentage of criminality in schools these days, that students have to be checked through security because an astonishing percentage of them carry lethal weapons. Check out the plethora of graffiti in urban areas. Check out the average age of gang members. Truly our youth has become much more a plague than a blessing. Unfortunate are the parents who decided to give birth to so many of these hellions. That is what I believe the Christ was referring to. Parenting is not for cowards. If you are going to be a parent, prepare yourself to enforce discipline or you will create a monster.

Furthermore, He does not say "happy is the womb that has not been penetrated." He does not criticize the practice of birth control which was very well known in His days and long before Him. He merely says that you would be much happier without children! Meditate on that.

Why was it so difficult for people to be born in the days of the Christ, at the time of that new dispensation, and today at the time of the New Age dispensation? Whenever a great influx of spirituality is expected from the Forces of Light, the forces of darkness send in a great influx as well. Consider the emperors who followed Augustus in the Roman Empire. The Christ lived in the days of Tiberius. Tiberius was a monster of sexual indulgence and cruelty. He was plagued by the ugliest possible diseases, as if cursed by God. The Island of Capri where he lived most of the time at the end of his reign was known for its orgiastic practices, its bestiality, and its wanton sado-masochism. Caligula, his successor, was equally horrible, if not worse. With Claudius, there was a hiatus of sanity. However, insanity picked up again with Nero who was next.

In this century we have been inflicted with the likes of Lenin, Stalin, Hitler, Mussolini, Mao Tse-Tung, Pol Pot and many others. Hundreds of millions of people have been tortured and killed. The degree and amount of cruelty in the twentieth century far surpasses that of past centuries. Indeed, one has to go back to the Roman Empire to find such extraordinary excesses. Alongside this are the great dispensations of the New Age such as Alice Bailey's Tibetan, Madame Blavatsky, the discovery of various manuscripts, including this very Gospel of Thomas.

# NUMBER EIGHTY-FOUR

*Jesus says: "He who has known the world has fallen into the body, and he who has fallen into the body, the world is not worthy of him."*

This so very much resembles Number Sixty-One that we could say exactly the same thing here. We will spare you the boredom of redundancy.

# NUMBER EIGHTY-FIVE

*Jesus says: "Let him who has become rich reign, and let him who has strength refrain [from using it]!"*

Becoming rich in Christ's terms is not merely a financial matter. One is rich when one "has." When you are fully conscious of what you have, of what you possess, of all of your blessings, then you are rich, you are self-aware.

Becoming rich is a process of removing poverty consciousness from yourself. This is true on the inner as well as on the outer levels. If you remove poverty consciousness, you will feel instantly rich and you will become rich eventually on the material level as well. It is those people who have become "rich" that deserve to have power.

Those who have power and who use it wrongly will lose it. This is abuse. Power should be wielded judiciously, as a last resort, when convincing does not work.

A person who is given power and who uses it too much will forfeit it. This is diametrically opposite to a person who is "rich." He who uses his riches enriches himself. There is no limit to using one's riches. All of one's riches have to be used. However, power is to be conserved, accumulated, and used judiciously. If not, it disappears. The more you use your power, the less powerful you will be. By contrast, the more you use what you have, the more you will have.

# NUMBER EIGHTY-SIX

*Jesus says: "He who is near me is near the fire, and he who is far from me is far from the Kingdom."*

I love this one! This is the dilemma of the person who wants to find the kingdom of God without the process of purification. Proximity to the Christ, i.e., to the brightness of the light, will burn you. What gets burnt must, at some point or another, be sacrificed anyway. However, the burning will hurt you to the degree you are identified with that which burns.

For example, if you harbour conceit, self-will or fear and you get close to a source of light, an enlightened being, your conceit, your self-will and your fear will stand out like sore thumbs. You will feel at best uncomfortable, at worst burnt, exposed! So you will withdraw from the light. However, in withdrawing from the light, you are also withdrawing from the kingdom of God. You draw yourself away from your own fulfillment.

Sitting with Curtis, on September 13, 1994, editing this material he requested "more, here" on this saying. The best example I can think of to illustrate the above two paragraphs is the experience that this group and most of all Curtis himself went through at the time of the passing of our friend Don Tharp. The following is an excerpt from Don's eulogy which explains as well as could be expressed the process of his death, since it was written about 48 hours after his passing.

"Don knew he was dying. It was clear when the doctor told him that he had advanced cirrhosis of the liver. It was clear to him intellectually. The emotional clarity came a little later when I urged him to express fully how he felt about dying. Huge resentment, huge screams came out of his already weak body. 'I did not plan to die so young,' he screamed. 'It is unfair,' he yelled. I asked him how he contracted hepatitis. At that point the screams collapsed into deep sobbing. He was clearly seeing that he had created the situation. It was clear to him that he was responsible for the destruction of his own liver through his own carelessness, his own egocentricity, and his own self-indulgence.

This whole emotional scene lasted about an hour. At the end of it, Don was in a state of grace. Not only had he accepted on the emotional level that he was dying, but he had also made the causal link between his actions and the destruction of his body. Emotionally, this made him accept his death because the universe was no longer unjust. He went through the pain of the fear of death which is nothing else but the pain of the fear of injustice. He came out on the other side of the pain in a state of grace.

Once that was done, we were able to tell him what we felt about his death, how we would miss him, how we had selfish feelings about it: Who would accompany us when our hymn was sung on Sundays? Who would play for us at the time of the offering, who would talk to me about music with the unique understanding that he had about the Baroque and the Rococo styles? There was a lot of joy and humour that followed this. Everybody was laughing about it, including him.

He remained in that state of grace until his last breath. His acceptance of death revealed to him the reality of eternal life. He experienced eternal life before dying. This was obvious to all of us who saw the light emanating from his eyes up until Monday, August 29th. On Tuesday, only the personality remained in his body. The soul had already left. Nevertheless, he was not suffering.

This clarity, which is achieved through courage and honesty, is what made possible a painless death, in spite of the massive destruction that was going on in his body. His courage and honesty was made possible by two years of working on himself to dissolve his pretenses, his masks, his misconceptions, his desire for approval, his vanity, his fastidiousness, etc. Not that he resolved it all. There is more work to be done and he is doing it as we speak.

When I met Don a couple of years ago, he was the epitome of the good guy, the accommodating person who wouldn't do anything that could hurt your feelings or ruffle your feathers. He was Mr. Equanimity. However, in reality this was merely a front. Behind it was a huge battle of which he was just semiconscious. You see, he craved approval because he had always felt unloved, rejected. He was in pain. He was in conflict between who he really was and who he desperately wanted to appear to be. He was, in reality, unconventional, an iconoclast, a revolutionary. Deep inside he did not subscribe to any of the ways of the little bourgeoisie. At the same time, he desperately wanted to appear to be as conventional and acceptable as you could possibly imagine. He tried to be as nicely dressed as he could. Not a hair was ever out of place. Not a negative word was ever said. He always smiled at everybody. He was unable to confront anyone, which complicated his life.

This conflict ate him up on the inside. All around him people contributed to this pretense by colluding with him, by encouraging his own rejection of himself. This was done not overtly, but covertly, with smiles, with giving of approval, without ever confronting him, or telling him anything that he did not want to hear. Those who did this were not helping him.

Had he not given up the pretense, he would indeed have died in great pain. He understood that compromising is not finding peace. It is denying that there is a war and perpetrating it at the same time. Those who live in pretense and those who encourage pretense in others cannot find peace. They, as Don did for the better part of his life, deeply reject themselves, have given up on themselves, are afraid to face themselves lest they find unpleasantness that they do not want to resolve. If they cannot find peace in life, they will not find peace in death. They will have great difficulties in accepting the reality of eternal life.

Don was hoping to somehow develop a ministry through his music and through the teachings of this church. I am convinced that this is what he is doing now, and that all that we have lost is being gained where he is now, in the kingdom of God."

# NUMBER EIGHTY-SEVEN

*Jesus says: "Images are visible to man, but the light which is in them is hidden. In the image of the light of the Father, it [this light] will be revealed, and his image will be veiled by his light."*

The first sentence of this saying brings to light (pardon the pun) many things:

1. The word "images" refers to what we call freezes, wrong conclusions, arrested and/or reduced conceptualizations, imitations of life. They exist in man because he has hidden his own light from himself. That is why the Christ spoke in parables, always presenting truths in reduced fashion so as to have people understand them. Nevertheless, images or parables try to imitate the truth but can never be the truth.

2. It also refers to people's propensity to look outside of themselves for causes and consequences, rather than making the connection with that which is within. This unfortunate mistake is the root of all problems. If we were to look within ourselves for the causes—positive or negative—of the events that occur to us, then our problems would be solved.

3. In order to perceive these images, some of the light must be shining through because in total darkness nothing can be perceived. It makes me think of the light that miners carry on their helmets which illuminates the part of the mine which is directly in front of them.

4. All images contain a grain of truth. This truth is increasingly revealed as the inner light is revealed.

In the second sentence we are told of the necessity of having a concept of the Father, i.e., of the Infinite. To the degree we can comprehend the reality of infinity, to that degree we become aware of the image of the light of the Father—not the full power of the light of the Father. For us, our image of the Absolute (the Infinite) is the image of the light of the Father. The cultivation of this concept—of the concept of infinity, of the Absolute, of divinity—is in itself a light. With the aid of this light, we are able to reveal our light, our divinity.

It is necessary to cultivate a sense of the Absolute and to bridge the gap between that which is absolute and that which is relative. It is extremely important to differentiate between the two. For instance, our three-dimensional universe is not perfect. We have to accept its relative nature and strive for perfection while accepting imperfection. This acceptance of the relative is contradicted by our lower self's demand for the Absolute here and now, which is an impossibility. Perfectionism, which is a human problem, stems from trying to make the relative be absolute.

On the other hand, while accepting and living in the relative world, we need to have our minds open to the Absolute and to its existence. We need to understand that everything stems from that absolute, including our relative world, and that it is only because of our misperception of the truth that we are stuck in the world of the relative. This acceptance, this cultivation of the Absolute is what the Christ calls "the image of the light of the Father." It is not quite the light of the Father, it is not quite the Absolute, it is our perception—the image—of the Absolute.

This perception of the image of the Absolute helps us reveal the light within us, the Absolute within us. To the degree I have a capacity to experientially accept and understand the Absolute, to that degree I will get closer and closer to my Higher Self. My image of God reflects precisely my development as a human being. The degree of the expansion of my consciousness corresponds precisely to the degree to which I have been able to experience the Absolute. In continuously trying to meditate on the nature and the reality of the Absolute, I expand my consciousness and, therefore, it is more possible for me to live successfully in the world of the relative.

"And his image will be veiled by his light"—the light is so strong that it is impossible for us to conceptualize Him in an image, to put Him in human words, or to depict Him in human terms, or with human technology. It is impossible to successfully reduce the Absolute in order to perceive it in the relative world. One has glimpses of it. The glimpses gradually become greater as our consciousness grows, but that is just about it. For the rest, we have to wait until we no longer need to reincarnate, until we have liberated ourselves of the necessity to live in the world of the relative.

# NUMBER EIGHTY-EIGHT

*Jesus says: "Now, when you see your appearance, you rejoice. But when you see your images which came into being before you, which do not die and do not show themselves, how will you be able to bear such greatness?"*

The Christ contrasts appearance with image. If we were to replace the word "appearance" with the word "mask," and "image" with "your Real Self," we would have the following: "Now when you see your mask, you rejoice. But when you see your Real Self which came into being before you, which does not die and does not show itself, how will you be able to bear such greatness?"

Your Real Self, your Higher Self, is your immortal self: it does not die. It does not show itself because you are too busy looking at your mask, being concerned with your appearance. As long as you are concerned about your appearance, you will not be able to bear such greatness as is contained in your Real Self, your Higher Self. To bear such greatness means to carry it, to manifest it the way Master Jesus carried the Christ consciousness. He bore Christ's greatness, and He died for the sake of this greatness. What are you willing to do for the sake of your greatness?

# NUMBER EIGHTY-NINE

*Adam was produced by a great power and a great wealth; but he did not receive (?) [...] worthy (?) of you, for he was not worthy [to (?)] be preserved from [being subject (?)] to death."*

What if we read it in the following way: "Adam was produced by a great power and a great wealth; but he did not receive these teachings which are worthy of you, for he was not worthy to be preserved from death."

This means that "you are worthy to be preserved from death." And indeed, they were, those people who listened to Him and who practiced what He preached. Besides, He knew He was going to fray a passage to the kingdom of God after His death which would then allow His disciples to make it, at least those who followed His teachings. This was indeed an innovation for humanity. Heretofore, since Adam, i.e., since the creation of humanity, they had been enslaved by the prince of darkness.

In this saying, the Christ is again trying to reduce His task as a saviour to vocabulary that could be understood by His audience. They were Jews, therefore, familiar with the Old Testament. The only way He could explain to them that since the beginning of consciousness human beings had been subjected to a fallen prince was to refer to the story of Adam.

Adam was not worthy because he was not ready. His acquisition of consciousness, eating from the Tree of Knowledge, marked his entrance into the long, dark tunnel. The emergence of consciousness, of awareness, had taken him out of the state of "being" and put him into a state of "becoming."

Initially in this state of becoming, salvation was not possible because it was blocked by the fallen being of light, the prince of darkness. And Adam entered the long, dark tunnel and could not see the light.

At the bottom of the tunnel, at the darkest time of humanity, on a winter solstice, light was born. Christ was born leading us up, out of the tunnel, into the light. The whole passage through the tunnel represents the state of becoming. When we reach that light, we are now back into a state of being, but this time with awareness. Christ frayed the liberating passage for all of us by demonstrating that it is possible to be tempted and challenged by darkness and still win.

# NUMBER NINETY

*Jesus says: "[The foxes] [have holes] and the birds have [their] nests but the Son of Man has no place to lay his head and rest."*

There is a connection between this saying and the previous one. It refers to the restlessness that comes from deciding to eat from the Tree of Knowledge, acquire consciousness, and enter the tunnel.

The foxes and the birds have not eaten from the Tree of Knowledge; they have no consciousness. This is what differentiates them from humanity and this is why they can rest their heads. They can sleep peacefully; they are still in a state of being. However, humankind is in a state of becoming; there is no rest in becoming—one continuously and perpetually struggles.

On a higher level, the Son of Man, if seen as the Christ Himself, finds no place to rest His head while others of much lesser development can rest peacefully. What is their nature? Foxes are wily and cunning; birds fly away and are unable to make commitments. It is the shiftiness and dishonesty in humanity that the Christ seems to be denouncing here. No one wanted to have anything to do with Him—His disciples all denied Him—He had "no place to lay His head and rest."

# NUMBER NINETY-ONE

*He said, he, Jesus: "The body which depends on a body is unfortunate, and the soul which depends on these two is unfortunate!"*

The body which depends not only on another body but on that which is physical, that which is material, that which is finite, is indeed unfortunate. This person is disconnected from infinity.

The soul which depends on (a) the body that houses it, and (b) this personality's materialism is unfortunate indeed. This person lives in duality. He does not see reality from the point of view of the unified soul, of the one soul. The process of unity occurs when the person starts seeing cause and effect relationships between soul and his material life.

Remember that the soul is not only positive. The soul is the seed in which is contained positive and negative. The individual who makes the connection between his soul and the material aspects of his life is causally connecting positive and negative occurrences with his innermost self, thereby unifying them.

In modern times, this should be taken a notch or two higher to the place of emotional or mental dependency. Instead of the word "body," if we were to put the word "emotion," we would have "the emotion which depends on an emotion is unfortunate, and the soul which depends on these two is unfortunate." The same thing here then applies on the emotional level. An emotion that depends on another emotion is indeed unfortunate because it is secondary. It will have trouble justifying itself. Only primary emotions can justify themselves.

Let's take an example. If anger comes as a result of fear, it will, at the same time, hate and depend on its maker. Its maker is fear. However, anger's nature is antithetical to fear. Indeed, it tries to repress it, to overcompensate for it, to negate its existence. At the same time, this particular anger is dependent on this particular fear for its existence, so it hates it but cannot do without it.

If you examine any of your conflicts, you will find them to be the consequences of those secondary states and reactions which are a great deal more distorted than the first one can ever be. In this particular example, a soul which depends on both the existence of the fear and of the anger for justification becomes a very unhappy one. The majority of humanity is imprisoned in dilemmas that resemble the one I describe here.

# NUMBER NINETY-TWO

*Jesus says: "The angels and prophets are coming to you; they will give you the things that belong to you. You, give them what you possess, and say: 'When will they come and take what is theirs?'"*

What we receive from the angels and the prophets are their teachings. They belong to us. They are meant for us. They are put in a way that we can understand. These teachings must be very personally and very intimately applied to every facet of our lives. We own them. It is not the type of thing that can be handled at arm's length. We must embrace what they give us, incorporate it.

We, in turn, must give them what we possess. Our material possessions must be put in the service of that dispensation, of the teachings that have come through. We also possess our time and our talents. These also must be laid at the feet of the angels and prophets.

I believe that the last saying, "when will they come and take what is theirs" refers to the process of death, of relinquishing. It corresponds to the great initiation of renunciation as experienced by the Christ on the cross. This is when the angels take what is theirs—our soul, which is angelic—out of our body.

This describes a continuous interaction, a give and take with the spirits of God. If you consider, for example, that the Law of Brotherhood is sharing, you will perceive through this saying an invitation to become part of the Forces of Light, part of Christ's hierarchy. Only in this total involvement can you help the ushering in of new teachings, can you find your task, can you find happiness and grace.

In the last sentence, do you sense this anxious feeling, this looking forward to dying? In those days, the only possible liberation was death, the end of the career, the removal of the soul from the body, the disengagement of the spiritual from the temporal. Today, it is different. We do not have to wait for death in order to manifest our soul here and now in the body. The Christ is claiming this kingdom here and now as being His. There is no longer a need to desire death as a liberation.

# NUMBER NINETY-THREE

*Jesus says: "Why do you wash the outside of the cup, and do not think that he who made the inside made the outside also?"*

This is a well-known saying of Jesus. He, of course, is referring to the process of purification. It is just as important to cleanse yourself on the inner level as it is to cleanse yourself on the outer level. The cleansing rituals that you go through on the outer level every day must be accompanied by just as thorough a cleansing ritual on the inner, more subtle bodies, such as your emotional and your mental bodies.

Once again, this is a strong indication of the Christ's emphasis on the process of purification. Once again, we emphasize that no process of growth, no religion, no path is valid unless it contains a continuous practice of this process of purification on the inner level.

Washing the outside of a cup does not limit itself in its symbolism to cleansing the body. It also refers to presenting a clean appearance as a mask. "I can use part of my emotional and mental bodies as clean fronts while hiding a lot of dirt behind them"—inside the cup. A thorough washing of the cup must be total. A thorough purification of an individual must be as equally complete. No stone can remain unturned. No dirt can be left unattended at any place in the entire entity.

To what extent do you practice that?

# NUMBER NINETY-FOUR

*Jesus says: "Come to me, for my yoke is excellent and my authority is sweet, and you will find rest for yourselves!"*

The yoke is His leadership. Christ's leadership is excellent, i.e., He will treat you fairly but still have you do your work. Compare to Matthew 11:29-30[6] where we get lost in all kinds of "meekness and lowly in heart" nonsense. In Matthew we also get to experience an "easy yoke," thus seducing us, encouraging our line of least resistance.

Why should we want an easy yoke? The yoke is nothing else but Christ's leadership through our own mistakes, our own evil. We want a good and precise leadership that will get us through all of our problems. An "excellent yoke" is also one that can be understood and appreciated. An "easy yoke" caters to the conditions that we put to God. "Dear God, I will accept your yoke if it is easy." This is nonsense! It also leads to mediocrity.

Excellence can only be found through non-compromise, through the continuous search for total fulfillment and total truth. The false balance that is sought by those who translated Christ's sayings which ended up in the Bible leads to a pseudo-equilibrium, a pseudo-life which at some point or other will encounter upheavals and will be destroyed. The seeking of excellent leadership can only lead to permanence and success. It is also the best form of protection against all

---

[6] Matthew 11:20-30 (KJV): Take my yoke upon you, and learn of me; for I am meek and lowly in heart: and ye shall find rest unto your souls. For my yoke *is* easy, and my burden is light.

of the calamities that we do not understand.

"My authority is sweet" refers to the Christ's love for His followers. If you surrender to the truth, you will find that authority to be sweet. If you resist it, as did the Romans and authorities in Palestine in those days, then Christ becomes a great threat, a rabble rouser, a destabilizer. So does any good authority.

To what extent are you able and willing to recognize true authority? To what extent are you able and willing to allow its yoke around your neck? Do not complain about attracting false teachers. You create false teachers; you draw them to you to suit your own line of least resistance.

"And you will find rest for yourselves," of course, refers to the rest that comes when the work is done. If you have surrendered to an excellent yoke and a sweet authority, then you will rest; if you have put in an honest day's work, then you will sleep the sleep of the just whatever your condition.

# NUMBER NINETY-FIVE

*They said to him: "Tell us who thou art that we may believe in thee." He said to them: "You examine the appearance of heaven and earth, but He who is front of you you do not recognise, and this moment you know not how to examine!"*

You, yourself, must recognize true authority and follow it. It is your responsibility. No matter how authority presents itself, whether it claims to come from heaven or from Earth, the form is not important, the choice lies solely with you. In the last analysis, it is the way you choose your teacher and it is also the way that you interpret his teachings that count.

The seeking of and the finding of a teacher is not an easy task. One has to really want to find a teacher, to have a deep longing for it. Then, when the teacher is found, there is a deep sense of instant recognition. The greater the degree of your consciousness, the more easily will you find your teacher and will you accept his leadership. The greater your desire to cheat life, to take from it more than you give, the more "you know not how to examine."

This last sentence also refers to the way you use your teacher. What questions do you ask? To what extent do you apply his teachings; to what extent do you take full advantage of his presence while he is there?

See also the commentary of Number Forty-Eight.

# NUMBER NINETY-SIX

*Jesus says: "Seek and you will find! But the things you have asked me about during these days and which I have not told you up till now, I now want to tell you, so that you will not have to seek them any longer."*

Sometimes a teacher will not tell you all he sees and will not give you all of the answers to your questions. There are many reasons for this. In the first place, he may want to let you discover them for yourself. The process of discovery, of seeking, should not be bypassed because the answer is experientially understood when one finds it by oneself.

In the second place, it is sometimes difficult for a follower to understand some of the answers given by a teacher. Material that is over his head, that he is not ready to receive, may take him away from focusing on what matters to him, here and now.

However, I get the sense that the Christ has decided here to impart some teachings that perhaps would be understood later. He did this probably because He sensed His imminent death.

"So that you will not have to seek them any longer," means whenever you seek them in the future they will be right there for you to refer.

Compare also to saying Number One. Those answers which astonish and make you wonder sometimes also scare you and blind you, another reason why they are not imparted to you fully.

# NUMBER NINETY-SEVEN

*"Give not that which is holy to dogs, in case they throw it onto the dunghill; and cast not pearls to swine, for fear that they should make it [...]*

In Matthew 7:6 we have a suggestion as to how this saying ends: "turn to attack you." If you give knowledge to those who are not ready to use it, they will turn against you and destroy you.

Why would anyone want to cast pearls to swine? To look good, to appear wise, to gain power, to make money.

This saying came in very handy for me today. A little earlier I was talking to someone who was interested in working with us on my consulting teachings. She was not interested in the purification process, only in the mechanics that make those who work with me successful.

While my consultant-follower was willing to give her what she wanted, I stopped him, requiring that (a) she be in a process of purification, and (b) only as a result of the purification work could she work with us at some future date on our methods of consulting.

I may have lost a client but I gained self-respect and I did not set up a situation that would boomerang against me later.

I pray always to have this integrity. Do you? Do you look for it? Do you cultivate it? Or do you run at the mouth, casting pearls to swine and giving that which is holy to dogs?

That which is holy must be treated as such, valued and dispensed judiciously, no matter what appears to be the temporary loss, no matter how many people feel rejected in the process.

# NUMBER NINETY-EIGHT

*Jesus [says:] "He who seeks will find, [and to whomever wishes to enter (?)] it will be opened."*

This can be compared to Matthew 7:7-8. I almost prefer it in Matthew: "Ask, and it will be given to you; seek, and you will find; knock, and it will be opened to you. For every one who asks receives, and he who seeks finds, and to him who knocks it will be opened."

This is the guarantee that every longing we experience will be fulfilled. Every soul movement will find its fulfillment, whether positive or negative, conscious or unconscious. Our life is, therefore, the sum total of all positive and negative soul movements in our entity. If you want to know what is inside you, look at your life and look at your body. They are every instant formed, again and again, by energy currents that you continuously repeat.

How much can we draw out of this? Plenty:

1. Do not stop longing, needing. Therein lies your power, since longing and needing are the most powerful currents in the universe. You might say, "I thought love was the most powerful force in the universe." You are absolutely right; it is. However, when you experience your longing and when you experience your needing, you are experiencing your love. Take, for instance, your prayers. When you pray to God, when you long for God's presence, aren't you then experiencing your love for God and aren't you expressing it through your longing? Take your longing for somebody with whom you are in love. By experiencing this longing aren't you expressing your love for him or her?

2. Do not transform your longing into demands; do not expect instant gratification. If you do, you will be propelled into despair, you will abandon your search, and you will never find fulfillment. The cycle will be repeated until you do find fulfillment in who knows what future incarnation.

3. The door is opened to him who knocks; knock on the door; knock loudly; take the Kingdom by violence; storm it; do not compromise.

4. Aggression is good. Keep going; yes, you can obtain all you want: all the happiness, all the bliss, all the fulfillment you will ever be able to imagine.

5. Do not wait for a door to be opened in order to knock on it. An open door is suspicious as well as specious. Those teachers who try to seduce you into following them are to be questioned. When you find the right teacher you will be in a position to ask him to help you, not the other way around.

6. If you combine this saying and the previous one, you can draw some interesting conclusions:
- You must seek the pearls in order for them to be given to you; you must want that which is holy in order to receive it; that is what true teachers are waiting for—your request, your search.
- If you do not seek, then you are no better than a swine or a dog. Stopping your search regresses you to animalism.
- Prematurely giving you that which is holy—the pearls—keeps you in a regressed, animalistic state since you do not exercise your longing to get those goodies.
- It is necessary to give value for that which you receive. Here we join saying Number Ninety-Two in which the Christ commands you to exchange what you possess for

what the angels and prophets possess. This is at the bottom of giving to churches, religious organizations, and philosophical establishments. You give to them to enable them to give you wisdom, spiritual truth—that which is holy, i.e., pearls.

To what extent do you give what you possess: your time, your money, your talents, your intelligence? Do you squander yourself on the universe? If not, why not? To what extent do you seek? How often do you question your belief system? What is your philosophy of life? Have you adopted the total philosophy of life in which you believe that the universe is just and that it is infinitely abundant, that love and truth are one with goodwill, that nothing happens out of chance or coincidence, that you have within you the power to be at-one with God?

If you content yourself with any lesser philosophy of life, you are not seeking, you do not wish to enter, you are not courageous enough to sustain the point of tension necessary for the door to be opened to you.

It is impossible nowadays for a true seeker to honestly believe that which is taught in organized religions or in schools of psychology. They are, at best, half-truths. Usually, they are outright lies. The only possible seeking must be done through yourself, through the deep questioning and rediscovery of the true nature of life within yourself. The only thing that differentiates humanity from animals is their spiritual seeking.

# NUMBER NINETY-NINE

*[Jesus says: "If(?)] you have money, do not lend it at interest, but [...] who(?) will not take them from him."*

What is money? It is an expression of value. It comes to you to the degree you give value. It enters your system and leaves you in accordance with your personality and soul.

What about those who are rich and misuse their money? How did they get rich? There is no haphazard occurrence in the universe. Those who have money, who are to the manor-born, who come into money, who make a lot of money, are experiencing now the effects of very positive efforts and behaviour that they manifested in earlier lives of their human career.

Unfortunately, they do not see their wealth as a result of what has happened in their past; they disconnect cause and effect. Furthermore, they do not want to see it; they want to believe that for no reason at all they were born in a privileged situation because they are intrinsically privileged. That, therefore, gives them the right to license. They do not have to work, they do not have to exert themselves, and still they get to have money. Their desire to abuse this money is itself an attempt at separating cause from effect and proving that there is no such connection. The more they abuse their money, the more they prove that they do not have to work for it. The more negative they are, the more they prove how privileged they are. Of course, this sets up a huge karmic debt. They are preparing now the conditions in which they will live their future lives.

One has to remember that in the days of the Christ there

was no inflation to speak of. Therefore, interest, which is a device to protect you from inflation, was unnecessary. Then, charging interest was a lot closer to usury than it is nowadays. I can see that it makes sense to charge an amount of interest that protects the owner of the money from devaluation through inflation. However, any more than this becomes greed and becomes usury.

Money is to be used for positive purposes. It is not there for your good pleasure, for your abuse, to keep you from working, to be a barrier to your task. This is what the Christ is trying to teach us when He directs us to lend money without interest and perhaps even give it away.

What is the point of having capital? If somebody who has a good cause can use capital and you have it, why not give it to him? You are not using it. Its presence merely keeps you dependent and debilitated and, therefore, corrupt. It prevents you from the healthy struggle that is necessary for you to accomplish your task, to use your talents.

This puts in question the entire concept of inheritance, of get-rich-quick schemes, and of using money for "protection." Protection against what? It only protects you against being of value to the universe which is no protection at all. As long as you are of value to the universe, money will keep pouring in.

Let's talk about the concept of welfare looked at from this point of view. If welfare is seen in the same way as is inheritance seen, then it is debilitating, it is abused as a continuous and perpetual reward for negative behaviour. Welfare should be a hand up from apathy and laziness, not a hand down into it.

If you are rich, to what extent do you still worship your bank account, your stocks and bonds, your coupons, etc.? If you are not rich, to what extent do you waste yourself in wishful thinking about lotteries, getting rich quick, or wishing for a rich and forgotten uncle to leave you a fortune? All of this is debilitating.

Give this up; give this out. Leave yourself naked and longing and you will discover your strength. You will be richer than you ever have been. Relying on inheritances, bank accounts, protection through money makes you feel continuously and perpetually poor inside. Only because you are poor inside do you need this outer level compensation. Rid yourself of it and you will feel your riches on the inner level which will then manifest as earned riches on the outer level, through your good work and through the re-enlivening of your instinctual needs.

The last part of this saying does not quite make sense. In other translations it is paraphrased as, "instead of lending, give it without expecting it back." If this is what He said, then it makes sense and corresponds to our above commentary.

# NUMBER ONE HUNDRED

*Jesus says: "The Kingdom of the Father is like a woman who put a little yeast [into three] measures of flour and made some big loaves with it. He who has ears let him hear!"*

Here we have again a link with abundance, with our fear of not having enough. The Christ gives us a key to always having abundance. The key is quality, which is represented here by the yeast. Quality, yeast, will make a little go a long way and will satisfy us and our hunger. Ultimately, it is quality that we seek, not quantity.

I also see here the symbolism of the penetration of the aspect of Mother/Matter, by the Will (Father), thus creating abundantly. If you let yourself be permeated by, impregnated by the Will aspect, the Father aspect, the One Initiator, you will expand, grow, and have abundance and experience pleasure and satisfaction. This also can be seen as the infusion of life into non-life, yeast being a living thing.

# NUMBER ONE HUNDRED ONE

*Jesus says: "The Kingdom of the Father is like a woman who takes a vessel of flour and sets out on a long road. The handle of the vessel broke: the flour spilled out on the road behind her without her knowing it and stopping it. When she arrived at the house she put the vessel down and found it was empty."*

This depicts the life of an individual. We start on the road of life full of our potentials and our talents. Somewhere on the road we lose control. This loss of control corresponds to the necessity to bring into your life the involuntary process and trust it. As we lose control, we scatter ourselves, we squander ourselves on the universe, we give of ourselves. We do so largely in an unconscious manner. We emanate stuff much more unconsciously than consciously.

At the end of our life, we arrive at our home, the Father's home, the kingdom of God, empty, having emptied out our task, having accomplished what we needed to accomplish and being ready for more. It would be tragic indeed to arrive home not having spent everything we needed to spend, not having manifested all of our potentials.

There is also the exact opposite interpretation. A person may go through his life losing his handle on his task and squandering everything he has without a focused intent or purpose. At the end of his life, he will feel empty and futile, having wasted all that he had and accomplishing nothing.

# NUMBER ONE HUNDRED TWO

*"The Kingdom of the Father is like a man who wants to kill an important person. In his house he unsheathed the sword and stuck it in the wall to assure himself that his hand would be firm. Then he killed the person."*

Of course, this saying has been omitted from the prudish, namby-pamby Gospels of the Bible. As I said before, Christ's words have been distorted to make Him appear to be non-violent, non-threatening, and, if anything, a victim. Nothing could be further from the truth. In this saying, as well as in many others, the Christ clearly recommends the use of violence in defense of one's home. Here, He clearly advocates readiness, unsheathing the sword and sticking it in the wall so as to have it readily at hand should the need arise.

On the physical level, there is here obviously a recommendation for physical violence, even military intervention when needed. Reread the Tibetan's message of June 30, 1940 quoted earlier in this book in Number Seventy-Eight. Henceforth, let no one believe that the Christ strictly advocated non-violence in the face of violence. This type of thinking belongs to the cowards of this world who hide behind pseudo-love.

The sword must be unsheathed, sharp, ready to cut mercilessly. This is as true for an individual defending his house as it is for a nation defending its territory and its citizens. This justified, sharp, and unequivocal defense comes—remember—from the representative par excellence of love! And don't you forget it!

The same is true on the emotional level. Unsheathing the sword means doing away with defensive mechanisms. The sharpness of clear and limpid emotions protects you while killing intruders and thieves, thieves of emotions. For more on theft of emotions please refer to the yoga sutras of Patanjali in which it is demonstrated that such a thing actually exists.

Perhaps a short word of explanation is in order here. One can be an intruder on the emotional level when one displays false emotions for the purposes of making oneself loved by another, i.e., intruding upon another's emotional body. This is also theft since the dishonest person robs another of his love. The process of purification, in which you confront your own manipulative emotional ploys, takes your emotional sword out of its scabbard and makes you ready to release your light which then slices through the dullness and darkness of manipulation.

Sharpness on the mental level is not unknown in our society. Mental clarity and sharpness provide you with the best possible steely defense, cutting through all the nonsense that comes at you. Mental sharpness is arrived at through the process of purification. Indeed, the cleansing of oneself of wrong conclusions brings one in touch with the limpid clarity of truth which cuts through and dissolves nonsense and uncertainty.

The "important" person is the lower self, or the Dweller, as it is called in the Tibetan's work. For humanity, it is Lucifer, the fallen angel. There is only one way to deal with that "important person," mercilessly, with steely sharpness and unequivocation.

# NUMBER ONE HUNDRED THREE

*The disciples said to him: "Thy brethren and thy mother are there outside." He said to them: "You and (?) those (?) who do the will of my Father, they are my brethren and my mother; it is they who will enter the Kingdom of my Father."*

This saying, along with Numbers Sixty and One Hundred Five, refers once again to the necessity to disconnect from one's physical family when one is on the Path. Time and again we have seen people who enter the Path develop conflicts with their physical families. Sooner or later the conflict is so great that a rift occurs. Entrance to the Path must bring destabilization of the existing status quo. In order for the individual to find his task, he must question everything which mother, brethren, and father have taught him. We have spoken about the necessity to go through this in Number Sixty.

Notice here that the brothers and the mother are not inside with Him. They are not part of those who are studying with Him; they are outside. Christ considers those who are doing the work with Him to be His real family. Therefore, all of those who seek to enter the kingdom of God through the process of purification belong to Christ's family.

At The Church of the Path®, we believe exactly the same way. It is a painful and inevitable reality that anyone who follows a Path of Purification will find himself in the same position as the Christ did, i.e., disconnecting from his physical family.

The necessity for disconnection also occurs with other relationships in one's life, for example, the strong friendships that exist with people who are not interested in following a Path of Purification. As the individual evolves on the Path, his contact with those who are not on the Path becomes more and more unbearable and impossible. A tearing ensues. It is not just with the parents that the separation occurs. It will occur whenever there is a difference between the rate of spiritual growth of people who are close to one another.

Another interesting point that emerges from this saying is the following: if Mary was such a holy person and if His brothers were such devout followers, what were they doing outside the temple? The Christ says essentially that they are not seekers of the kingdom of God.

This puts in question the worship of Mary. Mary was probably a very ordinary person who did not understand what her son was doing, just as our parents do not understand what we are doing on the Path. The worship of this unexceptional woman by the subsequent organized churches reveals their mediocrity. In some cases, there is so much adoration of the Virgin Mary that the Christ seems almost secondary.

I suppose it is a lot safer to worship an ordinary person who does not challenge you or threaten you than to worship the Christ who did, and does.

# NUMBER ONE HUNDRED FOUR

*They showed Jesus a piece of money and said to him: "The people who belong to Caesar ask us for taxes." He said to them: "Give to Caesar what is Caesar's, give to God what is God's, and what is mine give me!"*

It is interesting to note the removal of "and what is mine give me" from all the similar sayings in the four Gospels of the Bible.

Sayings such as this one demonstrate that He believed in the necessity to render unto Caesar. Jesus Christ was not against taxes. At the same time He also believed in the clear separation of church and state. What is Caesar's is Caesar's and what is God's is God's. We should not mix them. This was true and necessary in the days when government, money, and church colluded with each other shamelessly. Statesmen would consult oracles before making decisions. Oracles and priests were hopelessly intertwined with governments and kings. The separation of church and state was, therefore, a very necessary step in the right direction; it is still necessary and good since it protects freedom of religion.

However, in this new dispensation, the Spiritual Laws of ethics and the process of purification must penetrate every single area of human life, including and particularly the financial area. The light must shine on Caesar. The Spiritual Laws of money[7] must be applied; they are becoming clearer

---

[7] For further discussion on the laws of money, see the book, *Ethical Volition* by Rev. Dr. Albert Gani.

and clearer to humanity. Note that what is Caesar's is also God's. In this New Age, as Caesar's world is being penetrated by God's world, this becomes more and more a reality.

In saying "and what is mine give me," He points to three areas: (1) God, (2) Caesar and (3) Himself, i.e., (1) God; (2) material reality, active intelligence and adaptability, the ray of mother, three-dimensional reality, our daily bread, that which makes it possible for us to live a comfortable life; (3) Himself, representing the churches, the places of worship that need to be supported and maintained by the individual citizens.

In their short-sightedness, I guess those who deleted this phrase from the Bible did not see it that way. Otherwise, they would not have hesitated to leave it in. I suppose they were afraid to have Christ appear to be selfish. In actuality, He was demonstrating the rightness of healthy selfishness.

If you still have a problem understanding this, consider it from the point of view of the three Rays of Aspect:

1. Render unto Caesar (Ray Three the Mother). This is material reality which has to be respected, which has to be given to, which has to be recognized. The paying of taxes is a necessity without which the state cannot live. It corresponds to the recognition of the existence of our body and the necessity to feed it, to integrate it, to have pleasure, etc.

2. God (Ray One the Father). Here is where we have to render unto God the consideration of the existence of the Kingdom of Heaven, the laws of the universe which have their source in the spiritual. We render unto them by studying them, by practicing them.

3. Christ (Ray Two the Son), the Ray of Love and Wisdom which involves the giving to others, the manifestation of the

Law of Brotherhood which is sharing, being attractive and being attracted, as well as teaching others.

Those on Earth who intercede between God and humanity have to be recognized as representatives of the Christ, of the Second Ray. Christ here is asserting their existence and their position as essential contributors to the running of the universe. There is a link here with the Tibetan's teachings wherein he says that humanity (Third Ray) could not possibly receive and assimilate the dispensations as they come from Shamballa (The First Ray). They need the intercession of the Hierarchy (Second Ray, the Christ) in order for those currents dispensed by the First Ray to be assimilated and perhaps digested a little bit before they are finally given with love and the art of teaching to humanity.

# NUMBER ONE HUNDRED FIVE

*"He who has not, like me, detested his father and his mother cannot be my disciple; and he who has loved h[is father a]nd his mother as much as he loves me cannot be my disciple. My mother, indeed, has [...] because in truth she gave me life."*

Again, the same motif is repeated here. The bearing of your cross, i.e., the long dark tunnel through the *via dolorosa*, the path that leads to God, the accomplishment of your task must involve the **hate** of father, of mother, as well as of son and of daughter. See Matthew 10:37-38 and Luke 14:26-27.

Notice also that if anyone loves his father and mother as much as he loves the Christ he then cannot be a disciple either. The love that you have for your mother and your father, when projected on the Christ or any other teacher, is called in psychology **transference**. The problems of transference are clearly addressed here in the *Gospel of Thomas*. This problem was very well known to the Christ who denounces it as regressive and negative.

Take that, psychologists! If you think that you invented transference or if you think Freud did, you are indeed very much mistaken. All of this already existed in spiritual search. It is the property of the spiritual realm, not of the state, not of the board of certification, not of Caesar. Loving a teacher the way you love your mother or father—erroneously called positive transference (there is no such thing as positive transference, all transference is negative and hurtful)—must be experienced, recognized, identified and dissolved.

In the practice of our religion here at The Church of the Path® we do this continuously. We are thoroughly and deeply familiar with this process denounced here by the Christ.

By the way, do not forget detesting your children as well. The worshipping and idealization of children brings you to emotional and mental incest, let alone physical, of course, if you carry it that far. There are many ways of masking this incest, all of which are negative.

Notice, also, that Christ says here "he who has not, **like me**, detested...," thus admitting that He has gone through this process of having to detest the negative contracts that He Himself created with His parents. This means that He created evil within Himself when He was born, the same as every one of us. How could He possibly be our teacher without having experienced these very difficult problems? We believe that this is why He was sent by God, to create this evil inside and then to overcome it, thus demonstrating a true task in its completion.

The last sentence seems to be totally incomplete. Other translators of this Gospel have offered probabilities of its meaning that do not satisfy us at all.

# NUMBER ONE HUNDRED SIX

*Jesus says: "Cursed are they, the Pharisees, because they are like a dog which has lain in the cattle manger, but will neither eat [the food there] nor allow the oxen to eat it."*

This is reminiscent of all of the "Woe to you scribes, and Pharisees, hypocrites!" as found in Matthew 23 and Luke 11. In our day, the Pharisees are people in organized religions, people of the status quo, all of those people who call themselves professionals and who band themselves together in great monopolies to inflict on the populace their outrageously expensive services. The governments that support them are just as equally cursed.

Today, the Christ would have said, "cursed are you, senators, congressmen, presidents, popes, presbyters, cardinals, priests, preachers, lawyers, American Medical Association, American Bar Association, professional psychologists, professional counselors and all other related associations." He would have put in the same package all of those who sell their soul for a diploma or for maintaining the status quo.

All of the cowards that capitulate for money or for approval are the cursed Pharisees of today. You see them driving their Lexus, using their car telephones, parading in their latest clothes and glorifying how busy they are. In Luke, He even refers to lawyers, "Woe unto you lawyers," perhaps feeling lawyers are the worse offenders. Isn't it a bit the same today?

The evil that they do is described through this parable. The dog is a guard dog, somebody who wields power through the word (barking) or through regulations and who directs the cattle, i.e., the populace. The manger is obviously the place where one finds food and shelter, in this case spiritual food and spiritual shelter. It was also the place where He was born, thus, the place where you hunger for the new dispensation, Christ in you, is born.

The Pharisees prevent people from access to spiritual food, i.e., making Spiritual Law available to the people. They also "will neither eat the food" themselves. They themselves do not partake of the spiritual food.

Doesn't that sound like the accepted, conventional people who in their utter hypocrisy claim to be spiritual while never availing themselves of spiritual food in reality, never cleansing themselves, never embracing the process and never allowing anybody else access to spiritual food or the cleansing or the sheltering of the laws of God?

The outrageous and greedy ways practiced by these people is not limited to the spiritual. It extends to the material. On the material level, they prevent people from having money; they take money away from them. And on the physical level, these modern day Pharisees avail themselves of that money. They pile it up for themselves, they spend it as they please with complete disregard for the outcome of their actions.

Were they to avail themselves to spiritual food (purification) like they avail themselves to physical food (money), they would stop their hypocrisy, they would relinquish their power and they would live and let live along with the other inhabitants of the manger.

Once in a while a great upheaval comes around and cleanses all of this. If the dogs in the Soviet Union were toppled as easily as they were in the 1980s, I assure you that the dogs mentioned above will get their comeuppance sooner or later. All Pharisees will fall. The truth shall set us free. The truth is setting us free.

Note: Thank God there are honest doctors, lawyers, priests, etc. Eventually, they are the ones who are and remain successful. No success can be long-lived when it is based on hypocrisy and dishonesty. Let no one say that he cannot practice his trade in honesty. This is the height of nonsense. Any and all trades can and should be practiced in the spirit of truth and honesty. By and large, humanity has made great strides in that respect. In spite of what is going on today, we still live in a society that is more just than any that existed in antiquity.

# NUMBER ONE HUNDRED SEVEN

*Jesus says: "Blessed is the man who knows [where] the robbers are going to enter, so that he watches, he gathers his [...] and girds his loins before they enter."*

The entering robbers are those who manipulate and trick you. For the Christ they also include those people who tried to infiltrate His following for the sake of spying on Him.

Again, this motif of robbing should be compared to Patanjali's saying as in emotional theft and mental theft[8]. Patanjali makes a point of proving that theft can exist on the emotional and mental levels: you can steal an idea, you can steal a feeling.

Theft on the emotional level, for example, can involve the pretense to feel a certain way in order to get a person's approval. By doing so you are stealing this person's acceptance or love.

Many people try to steal our material and apply it in a diluted form. This is one thing you cannot do. In its diluted form it is no longer the same material. It does not have its sharpness. Without its sharpness it cannot heal. Any benefit obtained through it in its dull form can be compared to the benefits obtained through hearing a half-truth. It can be misinterpreted and is usually put to the service of evil.

Those who steal our material dilute it because they are afraid of its sharpness. They fear alienating those to whom they will dispense this material in its original and pure form.

---

[8] "When abstention from theft is perfected, the yogi can have whatever he desires." Patanjali, Yoga Sutra #37

Therefore, they are not interested in the welfare of those who receive the material. They are interested in selfishly taking advantage of the material and making it a tool for their own personal gain whether on the material level or on the emotional level through approval, etc. They steal it because they want to selfishly use it, and by selfishly using it they have to transform it and distort it. If their intentions are clean and they give it cleanly then they will identify the source of the material without having any problem about doing so.

When we dispense this material in its blatant sharpness, *we* become the beneficiaries anyway since it is our task to reveal this in its blatant sharpness and to encourage people to apply it to their lives.

To be prepared (to know where the robbers are going to enter), one has to make sure that one knows his own house very well and watches it very thoroughly. This surely refers to the uncovering and illumination of the unconscious, our inner house. Girding the loins, a clear reference to sexuality, reveals the Christ's awareness about the places where we are the most vulnerable. There are many colloquialisms that express this in colourful ways. The most powerful force and the most pleasurable one in the universe, sex, is also the place where we are the most vulnerable. By minding it, by girding it, by cultivating it, and by purifying it we protect ourselves against those who want to steal it or take advantage of it. Therefore, blessed is the man who knows his weaknesses and who minds them through the process of purification. He cannot be robbed.

# NUMBER ONE HUNDRED EIGHT

*They said [to him:] "Come, let us pray and fast today!" Jesus says: "What then is the sin that I have committed, or in what have I been at fault? But when the bridegroom comes out of the bridal chamber, then they must fast and pray!"*

In the corresponding sayings in the Bible (Matthew 9:14-15, Mark 2:18-20, Luke 5:33-35), we learn that the disciples of John the Baptist were questioning the ways of the disciples of the Christ. With John the Baptist you fast, you deny yourself, you repent. It seems as if with the Christ you do not do any of this. You enjoy yourself, as does a bridegroom, which obviously must refer to sex; I do not see what else it could be referring to when it says "when the bridegroom comes out of the bridal chamber," i.e., when sex has been consummated. Enjoy yourselves! Partake in the riches of life, **that includes sex!**

When you have had all you want, then fast. The process of fasting, i.e., cleansing, in no way denies or supersedes enjoyment or sexuality, or mutuality, as in "bridegroom," i.e., marriage. On the contrary, one enhances the other. Practice one correctly and you will be able to have the other just as correctly. There is a time to fast and a time to eat, a time to abstain and a time to have sex, etc.

There is also another level here. The Christ is the bridegroom. He urges people to enjoy themselves while He is present. Suffering will come when He goes away. And, sure enough, it did. Generally speaking, this is true about work that you do with a teacher. Enjoy yourself in his presence; take as much as you can from him because when he is gone you will be alone and you will fast; you will be hungry for spiritual food which you will then have to find on your own.

The hunger referred to, here, is a necessary phase ("they *must* fast and pray"). The hunger and the prayer are really the same, as they are both expressions of longing. Through this expression and through this experience, nourishment is found once again.

# NUMBER ONE HUNDRED NINE

*Jesus says: "He who knows father and mother shall he be called: 'Son of a harlot!'"?*

The word "knows" here obviously refers to intercourse, i.e., incest. Once again, the Christ refers to the incestuous relationship that one has with father and mother, not necessarily on the physical level. Fornication with father and mother occurs on the emotional and mental levels as well.

The process of formation of freezes, which is thoroughly explained in my book, *Know Thyself*, and in other places in my writings, is what is referred to here. He alludes to the sin of impressing mother's and father's distortions upon our soul substance. This is what constitutes the formation of freezes. He denounces this process as dishonest and illegitimate, clearly evil. That is why He calls it "son of a harlot."

The question mark here I interpret as "Should he not be called son of a harlot?"

# NUMBER ONE HUNDRED TEN

*Jesus says: "When you make the two one, you will become sons of Man and if you say: 'Mountain, move!,' it will move."*

This can be compared to Number Fifty-Three with the same explanation. However, this one is less allegorical in that it abstractly and personally says "when **you** make the two one, **you** will become sons of Man." It directly refers to the duality within one's self. It is also interesting to note here that the Christ is telling us that it is our task as sons of Man to achieve unity and, therefore, to acquire omnipotence—we will be able to move mountains once we achieve it.

# NUMBER ONE HUNDRED ELEVEN

Jesus says: *"The Kingdom is like a shepherd who has a hundred sheep. One of them, the biggest, went astray. He left the ninety-nine others and looked for this single [sheep] until he found it. After taking this trouble, he said to the sheep: 'I love you more than the ninety-nine [others]!'"*

This refers to the well known parable quoted in Matthew 18:12-13 and in Luke 15:4-7. I personally prefer the Luke interpretation. It clarifies several things:

1. That every single entity in creation will be saved.

2. That the focus should be given to the sinners or to the sinning parts of ourselves in an attempt to return them to the fold, i.e., save them. This motif is so applicable to our work on the Path. On the Path, we are not interested in focusing on those parts of us which have already made it, which are already positive, which are already free of trouble. We focus on those parts of us which are still sinning and we attempt to restore them to their original state.

In the process of redeeming them, the parts gone astray: (a) grow to be much greater than we ever thought they would be, and (b) help us become a great deal more than we ever thought we would become.

No task can be achieved unless the worst in us is made to be the best. That, too, explains why more love is given to the one sheep which goes astray. It is the worst that becomes the best. Far from injustice, this allegory points very powerfully to the process of transformation. The "biggest" sheep refers to the fact that it is in returning the negativities in us to their positive state that we accomplish our greatest achievements.

# NUMBER ONE HUNDRED TWELVE

*Jesus says: "He who drinks from my mouth will become like me. As for me, I will become what he is, and what is hidden will be revealed to him."*

This saying should be compared to Number Fourteen. Both of them refer to drinking, Number Fourteen "from the bubbling spring which is [the Christ]," and in this one, "from [His] mouth."

Drinking from the Christ's mouth means taking the words directly from Him in pure form without interpretation, without translation, without the terrible distortions that they have been subjected to. Drinking the pure words from the Christ will transform you and will make you become like Him. In no way does He place Himself in a superior position to us. He points out very clearly that we will one day become just like Him. This is our task, our duty.

Furthermore, it will make it possible for Him to manifest through you. Drinking His words from His mouth puts Him in our shoes. We then are restored to the state of nature and of at-onement with God. In that state, all of our unconscious becomes conscious. What is hidden is revealed. What is hidden in us is our unconscious. Here is again the link between becoming Christ-like (the ultimate healing of the soul and of the psyche), and the revelation of that which is hidden (the illumination of the unconscious).

So it is not merely a question of our becoming like Christ. It is also a question of Christ becoming like us. Each one of us will be a Christ. Each different human form will manifest and reveal Christhood in its own way. Christ will manifest in every possible area of human endeavour from business to religion, from art to the sexual act.

The reference to drinking connotes liquid. Liquid flows and adapts itself to the vessels that contain it. So it is with the spiritual material inhabiting us. It will take the form and the shape that we give it. It will express itself through our own fashion and our own words.

# NUMBER ONE HUNDRED THIRTEEN

*Jesus says: "The Kingdom is like a man who [has] a [hidden] treasure in his field and does not know it. He did not [find it before] he died, and he left his [property to his] son who did not know it [either]. He took the field, sold it, and the man who bought it went to till it: [he found] the treasure, and he began to lend at interest to those [whom he] wanted (?).*

Notice that in order for what is hidden to be revealed, there has to be an active component, a Christ-like component activated in the unconscious, below the unconscious as a matter of fact. This points to the essential role played by the Higher Self in the resolution of unconscious problems. This also points to the aspect of consciousness that exists in the unconscious and beyond it in the Higher Self.

That which psychologists call complexes are autonomous constellations of unconscious elements that have their own consciousness, that make up their own mind, that have their own will, that have their own Instinct of Self-Preservation, and that have their own idea of what is happiness and what is pleasure, albeit distorted.

One has to initiate a conversation with those unconscious places in oneself. For that, one has to allow the Christ to be born inside one's self. The conversation is then undertaken: (a) by the Christ within and (b) by the persona on the outer level that makes the process available. The persona, or the little ego, on the outer level is a reduced representation of the Higher Self or of the Christ found within.

Drinking from the Christ's mouth (saying One Hundred Twelve) awakens the Higher Self the way you would awaken the persona of an individual who then actively and deliberately undertakes the work of converting the other autonomous "complexes" that exist in the unconscious.

Eventually, a passage is frayed and it becomes possible for the inner Christ to contact the outer persona. This is when the task of the individual becomes activated on the outer level. Ultimately the Christ and the persona become one. In the Tibetan, this is explained as the process of the soul becoming one with the personality, thus completing the task of the individual on the level of human existence.

Identifying the Christ with the soul is not a novel idea. The soul is the second level within, the link between spirit and personality.

"The Kingdom is like a man who has a hidden treasure in his field and does not know it." The treasure is the potential to be found in our dormant unconscious. It is also the potential in our lower selves. Many of us on the Path are saddened by our parents because it is clear to us that they are far from discovering the treasure that exists in their unconscious, in the resolution of their lower self.

In this parable, the father dies without ever discovering the treasure that is buried in his field. The son who inherits the treasure seems to behave very much like the son of a rich man. He uses his inheritance for instant gratification, not bothering to dig in and see what is in there. He liquidates it. He sells the field to a man who takes the trouble to look into it.

There, in the dirt, the new owner discovers the treasure. Once the treasure is found, unlimited possibilities are open to the owner who lives off the interest, or lives off the way in which he puts the treasure to work. This leads to several conclusions:

1. Dig into your unconscious and you will find treasure in the places where you least expect it, i.e., in that which is the worst in you, in the dirt. See Number One Hundred Eleven.

2. Most people do not realize the treasures they possess. They take them for granted, abusing them for their own instant gratification.

3. Others who are more evolved will eventually do the work required to find the treasure and can then enjoy it along with the rest of the universe.

This parable is very reminiscent of Aesop's fable[9] which goes something like this: A man leaves a field to his sons, telling them just before he dies that a treasure is to be found buried in it. The sons dig up the entire field. They dig so thoroughly and so well that the earth becomes very fertile and yields a wonderful vineyard. This, then, is their treasure, the product of their labour to which they were led by their father's false pretenses.

Very often we are engaged in difficult tasks, laborious circumstances, not knowing why we do these things. Only in retrospect do we realize the value of this seemingly unnecessary labour. It is as if there was a guiding hand leading us to our task without our even knowing it.

This also points to the fact that a person's task is very seldom what he consciously believes it is going to be. The latter course of events often has absolutely no resemblance to what was pursued in the first place. This has been true of my life's circumstances as well as those of many people I

---

[9]The Farmer and His Sons, Fable #73

have known.

# NUMBER ONE HUNDRED FOURTEEN

*Jesus says: "He who has found the world and become rich, let him renounce the world!"*

This points to two requirements of the career of an individual:
1. To find the world, to create abundance for oneself, to live life to the fullest, to enjoy it, to drink the cup of karma to the last drop.
2. The necessity to renounce the world, having found it. If we do not renounce it, we will be stuck in it and we will never find out how much more pleasurable it is to live in infinity, in the Absolute, in the kingdom of God.

This renunciation refers to the fourth initiation. Knowing the world and becoming rich refers to the third initiation. Both initiations are amply explained in the Tibetan's and Alice Bailey's work. They are part and parcel of the career of an individual on this Earth sphere. Many successful people can be recognized as having gone through the third initiation of transfiguration.

If we consider Churchill and Roosevelt, for instance, we recognize the mark of the transfigured personality in contradistinction to those multitudes of mediocrities that we have known since then.

The inability to pass through the next initiation, which is the Renunciation, creates the incredible sufferings that I believe Howard Hughes went through, for example. Jesus, on the cross, went through the fourth initiation. Even He did not do it very elegantly, doubting the existence of God at the end.

The premature renunciation of the world creates what Uta Ranke-Heinemann calls "the eunuchs for the Kingdom of Heaven." She, an eminent professor at a Catholic university in Germany, demonstrates the incredible unreality of having celibate people deal with the problems of sexuality in humanity. It is impossible for anyone who submits himself (herself) to the self-imposed castration of celibacy to know anything about problems, trials and tribulations, joys, ecstasies, despairs, and pains of those of us who are involved in a full sexual life.

You cannot renounce life before you have lived it. You have to live it first before you renounce it. You cannot let go of anything unless you have accomplished it. You cannot let go of anybody unless you love them. You cannot let go of anybody whom you hate. At the same time, the ever-changing evolutionary process requires that you let go of that which has been accomplished and open yourself to higher work.

The defense against change creates incredible problems of inefficiency. Even in management, this is very well known. A person who has reached a certain level of proficiency in a particular position has to abandon it and learn a higher position. Otherwise, the entire organization is clogged.

Do you hold on to something that you have mastered, trying to make it the answer to all your problems, the source of all your goods? Do you rest on your laurels? If you do, crisis will come to you. You must relinquish.

# NUMBER ONE HUNDRED FIFTEEN

*Jesus says: "The heavens and the earth will open (?) before you, and he who lives by Him who is living will not see death," because (?) Jesus says this: "He who keeps to himself alone, the world is not worthy of him."*

Let's first explain each phrase as it is given in the saying:

1. "The heavens and the earth will open before you": this obviously speaks of cataclysms, of great storms during which the sky seems to open and there are floods which come forth and engulf the earth, or the earth opens as it does during great earthquakes or volcanic eruptions.

2. "And he who lives by Him who is living will not see death." Living by Him who is living means living by the laws of life. He who is living is the eternal youth, God. The laws of life are the Spiritual Laws. He who lives by those laws, i.e., by Him, has found immortality, cannot die.

3. "Because" means that there is a causal connection with

4. "He who keeps to himself alone, the world is not worthy of him." The person who is self-alienated does not live by Him who is living. Self-alienation, by definition, takes you away from Spiritual Law, away from God who is living. Keeping to yourself will, therefore, make you vulnerable to cataclysms. Vulnerability to cataclysms is a causal result that comes from disconnection from Spiritual Law, disconnection from the world.

This connects vulnerability to cataclysms with self-alienation. Let's see if we can guide you through that connection:

1. He who keeps to himself alone alienates himself from the world. However, eventually he will have to be integrated into that world. So,

2. The heavens and the earth will open before him and the person who has been alienated will find death. But the person who has been integrated will not see death. The cataclysmic event of heaven and earth opening up to him will be a blessing rather than a calamity.

This makes me think of all of the calamitous predictions that everybody, particularly New Agers, talk about with such great relish. They love boasting about their knowledge of great impending dooms. They love the power that predictions give them. The same can be found with the bigots in conventional religion who love to talk about the cataclysms as they are predicted in the Bible with the Gogs and the Megogs.

**None of them are living by Him who is living.** All of them are violating Spiritual Law. All of them are alone, alienated from the rest of the world. Here they are and there is the cataclysm that will finally integrate them into the world by hook or by crook, by death if necessary.

The cataclysm is merely the expression of their unresolved primitive self which they have so successfully repressed within themselves that it is now projected onto the outside world. Their vulnerability to these cataclysms is a direct result of their self-alienation from (a) their primitive self and (b) from the laws of God.

The alienation from the worst in you also corresponds to the alienation from the best in you.

# NUMBER ONE HUNDRED SIXTEEN

*Jesus says: "Cursed is the flesh that depends on the soul, and cursed is the soul that depends on the flesh!"*

The Christ here is talking about two extremes, two extreme characterologies. In our system, it is the two extremes found between Ray Six on the one hand, and Rays Five and Seven on the other.

With Ray Six, the flesh depends on the soul. In other words, the person is over-concerned about inner level occurrences, while disregarding, minimizing, and denigrating all of those happenings on the outer level. Here you have the mystic, the monk, etc.

Conversely, the soul that depends on the flesh gives you the Rays Five and Seven characterological types which are the ones concerned with concrete knowledge and science, with order and ceremony, respectively. They are concerned with things on the outer level, with their physical appearance, with the amount of money or goods they have. They are those who subjugate the soul to the outer level. The soul will be minimized, denigrated and disregarded. The outer level reality will be deified and glamorized.

Both extremes are cursed. They are both distortions. Today, late in the twentieth century, and late in the reign of Christianity, I wish those people who call themselves followers of Christ would heed this particular message a lot more seriously than they do.

Once again, this saying has been totally omitted from the Gospels of the Bible—and we know why, don't we?

# NUMBER ONE HUNDRED SEVENTEEN

*His disciples said to him: "On what day will the Kingdom come?" "It will not come when it is expected. No one will say: 'See, it is here!' or: 'Look, it is there!' but the Kingdom of the Father is spread over the earth and men do not see it."*

This saying corresponds to our beliefs. The kingdom of God is here and now. It is everywhere. It is actually a state of mind, as it were, or a state of the psyche. It is the degree to which you are free of your lower self. To that degree, you already live in the kingdom of God. You are already protected against all calamities. You are already experiencing ecstasy.

This is an attack on several things:

1. On the idea of heaven and hell to be found after death, which is a primitive idea that has seen better days.

2. The expectation of either a cataclysm or of a saviour who will come and change our life conditions to suit us. This reminds me of some limited bigots in the 1980s who were convinced that God would appear and, in an Armageddon-like battle, destroy the Soviet Union.

3. It removes all magical thinking and all necessity for reliance on outer level methods of healing. It brings us back to ourselves. **We** create or uncreate the kingdom of God on Earth. We inhabit it or we do not, depending on the degree to which we have evolved our consciousness.

The kingdom of God is here, it is your natural state! Divest yourself of all of that which is unnatural and you will recover the kingdom of God; you will be reborn in it.

# NUMBER ONE HUNDRED EIGHTEEN

*Simon Peter says to them: "Let Mary go out from our midst, for women are not worthy of life!" Jesus says: "See, I will draw her so as to make her male so that she also may become a living spirit like you males. For every woman who has become male will enter the Kingdom of heaven."*

Let's try to put aside our political correctness for a moment. When this saying was uttered, the symbol of femininity was the symbol of finiteness, of matter; masculinity, in contradistinction, was a unified principle that brought the finiteness of matter back to life.

Peter is known for his sexist hostility towards Mary. This appears quite a bit in other Gnostic literature. The antipathy for women is also found in Paul. I Corinthians is full of statements from Paul saying that women should not attend temples, and if they do they should be silent, cover their heads, etc. Paul further states in I Corinthians 11:3, "But I want you to understand that the head of every man is Christ, the head of a woman is her husband, and the head of Christ is God."

Therefore, ladies, you are at the bottom of the heap: first comes God, then comes Christ, then comes man, then comes woman. The distances between all of these states are equal. That is just about the only thing equal to be found in I Corinthians when it comes to sexuality.

I do not believe that the Christ was a sexist. He was trying to find a way to change these people's minds about women. He was trying to symbolically demonstrate that matter is dormant energy. The conversion of matter to energy is what is referred to here as "draw[ing] her so as to make her male," so that she also may become a living spirit like you males. The male is the living spirit. Matter is not; it is dead and it must be brought to life.

All matter has to be brought back to life. In our new dispensation, one finds many more female teachers, women channels, than men. Consider H. P. Blavatsky, A. A. Bailey, and Jane Roberts. As the pendulum swings, it is time for woman's receptivity to take the role of the dispenser of wisdom. Gone are the days of little child women obeying men. If anything, what we find these days is the exact opposite distortion, little boys obeying mother goddesses.

It is not necessary to unthinkingly follow what was said two thousand years ago. One has to see it from the evolutionary point of view. If we were to put this saying into today's vernacular, it would read something like this: "I will draw macho males so as to make them more receptive and so that they may become living channels like you females. For every male who has become receptive and female will enter the Kingdom of Heaven." This, then, re-establishes the balance.

Every man has a women within himself and has to integrate—become—that woman without losing his identity as a male. Conversely, every female has to integrate—become—the man within herself without losing her identity as a woman.

# CONCLUSION

Thus ends a very enjoyable commentary on Thomas. May this be a guiding book for all who read it. At the same time I pray that it not be dogmatized as so many other writings have. In an ever-changing universe, truths must be continuously expressed in new and more alive ways. Words, which are man-made, lose their power and their meaning when they are repeated over and over again.

Take the spirit of what is written here and apply it to your life. That with which you disagree gently put away, keeping your mind open to it. That with which you agree, apply to your life and let it make you happier, i.e., closer to Christ and to God.

"Let him who seeks cease not to seek until he finds...."
Gospel of Thomas #1

# INDEX

**-A-**
Absolute, The
   concept of, 37
Abundance
   creating, 270
   key to, 192, 242
   poverty consciousness, 96
   renouncing, 270
Abuse
   attracting, 113
Addiction
   creation of, 93
Alcoholism
   healing of, 94
Alienation, 272
Approval
   deadening by seeking, 170
   relinquishing, 41
Astrology
   danger in, 67
Atlantis
   knowledge during time of, 125
Authority
   challenged, 132
Awareness, 174

**-B-**
Backstabbing, 89
Being and Becoming, 222, 224
Belief
   blind acceptance, 143
Birth
   conditions of, 166

Blind
   leading blind, 111
Body
   dependency, 225
   subtle, 229
Brotherhood
   teachings on, 88
Business
   service in, 198
   success, 192
Byzantine Empire
   Arab negotiations, 208

**-C-**
Cataclysm
   expectation of, 275
   protection, 272
Catholic Church
   baroque decor, 15
   Counter-Reformation, 14
   Ignatius of Loyola, 14
   Jesuits, 14
   pageantry, 207
   reincarnation erased, 163
   rituals empty, 33
   sale of indulgences, 13
Cause and Effect, Law of, 218
   results of disconnection, 97
Change
   impeding, 271
   perpetual, 127
Channel
   closed, 121
   developing a, 87

Characterology
- exaggerations, 274
- life phases, 27
- Ray V, 274
- Ray VI, 274
- Ray VII, 274

Charity
- dishonest, 57

Child
- approval seeking, 167

Chosen, The
- teachings on, 83

Christ
- death predicted, 185
- humility of, 53
- incarnation, 195
- light personified, 205
- manifesting, 159, 264
- perfection of, 27
- preparation for the, 155
- revolutionary teachings, 64
- strength, 244
- task of, 154, 222, 230
- teachings in gospels, 11

Christianity
- God transcendent, 22
- immanence, 206
- replaced Roman system, 106
- Roman Empire, 156
- transcendence, 206
- worthless sinner distortion, 21

Christians
- condemnation of, 54

Church of the Path, The
- beliefs, 11

Churchianity, 146

Churchill, Winston
- transfiguration, 270

Civilization
- destruction of, 208

Cleansing
- inner, 229

Commitment
- spiritual butterfly, 201

Complexes
- psychological, 266

Compromise, 196
- relinquishing, 41

Confrontation
- rules of, 172

Conventional Religion
- rituals and superstitions, 33

Copernicus
- condemnation of, 54
- discovery repressed, 107

Coping
- relinquishing, 41

Counter-Reformation
- meaning of, 14

Cowardice
- pacificism, 199

Credentials
- slavery to, 164

Crucifixion of the Ego, 7, 168

-D-

Dark Ages
- knowledge concealed, 124

Death
- concept of, 152
- disciple facing teacher's, 49
- fear of, 16
- liberation at, 136
- meeting Being of Light, 98

*A Commentary on the Gospel of Thomas*

Death (continued)
    understanding, 66
Destroying
    negativities, 195
Disciples
    described by Jesus, 73
Discovery
    encouraged by Christ, 58
    repressed, 107
Discrimination
    right, 111
Doresse, Jean
    translator, 11
Doubt
    honest, 143
Duality, 147, 148, 261
    example of, 46
    lower and higher, 45
    teachings on, 80
Dweller on the Threshold
    defined, 36

-E-

Ego
    crucifixion of, 7, 168
Episcopal Church
    Curseo movement, 145
Ethics
    teachings on, 92
Evil
    impairs progress, 7

-F-

Faith
    loss of, 35
Fall, The, 222
Family
    breaking ties, 246
    ties, 165, 251

Fasting
    meaningless, 56
    teachings on, 90
Fear
    poverty, 242
    problem of, 24
Fire
    burning dross, 214
    setting your world on, 41
Forces of Light and Darkness, 7
France
    kings of, 129
Freeze, 218
    crystallized truth, 7
Freud
    condemnation of, 54
Friends
    breaking ties, 246

-G-

Galileo
    condemnation of, 54
Generosity
    poverty and riches, 128
Genius
    hated, 190
Get-Rich-Quick Schemes, 240
Giving
    motivation behind, 138
    teachings on, 88
Glamour
    exaggeration of divine, 7
Gnosticism
    distortion of, 125
    God is unconscious, 22
God
    concept of the Absolute, 37
    defined by Christ, 61
    existence in karma, 13

God (continued)
    finding inner, 153
    how to see, 117
    knowing self to find, 23
    looking inside for, 20
    nature of, 119
    search for, 167
Government
    evil of, 253
Gratitude
    lack of, 159
Greed, 203
Growth
    impeding, 271
    spiritual, 62

**-H-**

Hall of Knowledge
    entering, 123
Harmony
    found through conflict, 62
Healing
    awareness brings, 31
    self, 275
Heaven, 275
Hell, 275
Herd Instinct
    divine consummation of, 18
Hierarchy, The, 8
Higher Self, 8
    contacting, 204
History
    benefit of studying, 97
Hoarding, 192
Holy Spirit
    blaspheming, 135
    mother principle, 135
Humanity
    dishonesty of, 224

Hunger, 191
Hypnotism
    shortcut to healing, 31

**-I-**

Idealized self,
    Karen Horney, 8
Idolized Self, 8
    Real Self versus, 221
Ignatius of Loyola
    Counter-Reformation, 14
Image, 218
    freeze, 8
Immortality, 221
    finding, 43
    knowledge of, 68
    tasting, 66
    truth as eternal, 71
Incest, 260
Indulgences
    sale of, 13
Inheritance, 196, 240
    corruption from, 129
Initiation
    Dweller on Threshold, 36
    Fourth, 270
    Third, 270
Innovator
    hated, 190
Inquiry Instinct
    divine consummation of, 18
Instincts
    divine consummation of, 18
Integrity, 207

**-J-**

Jesuits
    Counter-Reformation, 14

Jesus
    castration of, 176
    sexuality, 176
John the Baptist
    importance of, 140
Judgements, 89
    cleansing, 55
Judiasm
    circumcision, 161
Justinian
    reincarnation removed, 163

### -K-

Karma
    results of disconnection, 97
    wheel of, 96
Kingdom of God
    finding, 275
Know Thyself, 188
    one-onement with God, 23
Knowledge
    inner, 188
    pearls to swine, 234
    quest for, 224

### -L-

Labor
    seen as pain, 173
Lavosier
    saying of, 187
Law of Brotherhood, 196, 227
Law of Cause and Effect
    denied, 218
    results of disconnection, 97
Lawyers
    evil of, 253
Laziness
    waste in, 77

Life
    conditions of, 166
    purposeful, 243
    self-protection, 114
    task, 173
Light
    burning of, 214
    manifestation of, 149
    teachings on inner, 87
Line of least resistance, 230
Longing, 236
    denied, 181
Lottery
    harm of winning, 57
Louis XIV
    understood poverty, 129
Louis XV
    abuse of wealth, 129
Louis XVI
    beheading of, 129
Lower self, 8
    integrate and convert, 35
Luther, Martin
    effects of, 14

### -M-

Maligning, 89
Mary
    worship of, 247
Mask, 9
    Real Self versus, 221
    teachings on, 115
Mastery
    obtaining, 18
Materialism, 131, 184
    burden of, 203
Middle Ages
    sale of indulgences, 13

Misceptions
    adopted, 45
Mobility
    versus rest, 151
Money, 239
    purpose of, 240
    pursuit of, 203
Mother-Father Split, 9
Motherhood, 209
Movement
    relaxation versus, 151
Mustard seed parable, 72

-N-

Nature
    restoring, 264
Need, 191
    denied, 181
    instinctual, 18
Neoplatonism
    teachings of, 52
Nero
    burning of Rome, 41
New Age, 145
    danger in predictions, 67
    excesses of, 210
    refreshing of concepts, 64
    role of women, 276
    spiritual butterfly, 201
    teachings of the, 16
Non-violence, 244

-O-

Origen
    advocate of knowledge, 125

-P-

Pacifism
    cowardice euphemized, 199

Paganism
    God is unconscious, 22
Parable, 125
    cornerstone, 187
    field of treasure, 266
    invitation to feast, 183
    lost sheep, 262
    merchant and pearl, 203
    rich man without need, 181
    sowing weeds, 171
    vineyard cultivators, 185
Paradise, 275
Parents
    hatred of, 165, 251
    independence from, 209
    ties, 165
Passers-by, 131
Past life
    wealth, 239
Path of Purification, The
    entering, 201
    family ties, 246
    few workers, 198
    fire of, 214
    longing for, 236
    psychotherapy versus, 150
    readiness for, 179
    regression, 222
    spiritual butterfly, 201
    unending search, 151
    ushering in, 227
Paul, Saint
    sexism, 276
Peace
    Christ brings a sword, 62
    finding inner, 153
Pearls to swine, 234
Perfectionism, 17
Persecution, 191

Peter the Apostle, Saint
   sexism, 276
Philosophy
   religion versus, 52
Physical Level
   exaggerated, 274
Plan of Salvation, 9
Pleasure, 258
   joy of life includes, 56
Possessions, 227
   meaning of, 128
   slavery to, 164
   ties to, 131
Poverty
   creation of, 24
   fear of, 242
Power
   abused, 213
   corruption of, 130
Prayer
   honest, 57
   meaningless, 56
Predictions
   danger in, 67
Procreation Instinct
   divine consummation of, 18
Profession
   greedy, 253
Prophet
   unaccepted in own city, 104
Psychology
   complexes, 266
   personal development, 12
   spiritual endeavour, 29
Psychotherapy
   versus the Path, 150
Purification
   humbling process, 141
   inner, 229

Purification (continued)
   lack of commitment to, 21
   personally applied, 227
   ploughing the soul, 72
   psychotherapy versus, 150
   wrong motives, 150

**-R-**

Rays of Aspect, 9
   harmonized, 102
Reformation
   meaning of, 14
Regression, 222
Reincarnation
   removed from Bible, 163
   wheel of, 96
Relationships
   finding unity, 178
Relaxation
   versus movement, 151
Religions
   philosophy versus, 52
   preparation for Christ, 155
Relinquishing, 205
Render Unto Caesar, 248
Renunciation
   premature, 270
Rest
   seeking, 175
   versus movement, 151
Riches
   corruption of, 130
   protection of, 181
Rituals
   meaningless, 56
Roman Empire
   Christianity, 156
   excesses of, 210
   morality of emperors, 129

Roman Empire (continued)
    Nero, 41
    reincarnation erased, 163

-S-

Sabbath, The
    teachings on keeping, 90
Sagittarius
    goal setting, 144
Salome, 176
Salvation,
    obtaining, 13
    Plan of, 9
Sanat Kumara, 119
Saviour
    expectation of, 275
Seeker, 17, 236
    spiritual butterflies, 38
    spiritual growth found, 62
    spiritual search of the, 37
    teachings on, 92
Self
    Distorted, 7
    Divine, 7
    Higher, 8, 205
    Idealized, 8, 221
    Lower, 8, 9, 35
    Mask, 9, 115, 221
Self-Assertion Instinct
    divine consummation of, 18
Self-Preservation
    divine consummation of, 18
Self-protection
    approaching life, 114
Selfishness
    healthy, 249
Separation of Church and State, 248

Service
    business, 198
Seven Rays, 9, 26, 102
Sex Instinct
    divine consummation of, 18
Sharing, 192
    true, 197
Simplicity
    ignorance euphemized, 124
    teachings of childlike, 79
Sin
    distortion of sinner, 21
    lost sheep, 262
Skill
    mastering a, 18
Soul
    what is, 225
Spirituality
    exaggerated, 274
    false, 254
Stinginess, 193
Students
    described by Jesus, 73
Sword
    Christ brings the, 62
    harmony found through, 62

-T-

Tarot
    danger in, 67
Task, 243
    accomplishment, 16
    activation of, 267
    discovery of, 186, 190
    life, 173
Taxes, 248
Teacher
    authority challenged, 133

Teacher (continued)
    death of a, 49, 77
    described by Jesus, 73
    devotion to a, 53
    finding the right, 133, 232
    healthy detachment, 104
    insights from a, 233
    longing for, 236, 258
    recognizing a, 61
    taken for granted, 121, 174

Teachings
    abundance, 128
    attacks and protection, 75
    authority challenged, 132
    Christ a revolutionary, 64
    conceit and inflation, 140
    creation of good and evil, 137
    death, 152
    ethical bedrock, 106
    goal setting, 144
    growth, 127
    guidance received, 109
    healthy detachment, 104
    Holy Spirit blasphemed, 135
    honest questioning, 143
    how to see God, 117
    hypocrisy, 144
    ignoring the Messiah, 134
    infinite dwelling in the finite, 101
    kingdom of God within, 153
    knowledge monopolized, 123
    limiting your capacities, 112
    masks worn, 115
    materialism, 131
    movement and rest, 151
    personally applied, 227

Teachings (continued)
    prophet in own city, 104
    purification, 140
    Rays of Aspect, 102
    readiness, 179
    repetition diminishes, 64
    reviving, 64
    search of God, 100
    self-protection, 114
    sharing and spreading, 39
    sharpness of new, 41
    spreading light, 149
    strength exulted, 112
    unity and duality, 147, 148
    valuing, 234
    worldliness, 114

Television
    exposure to violence, 59

Tertullian
    beliefs of, 125

Tharp, Don
    eulogy of, 214

Theft
    attracting, 113
    levels of, 256

Thomas
    who was, 11

Tibetan, The, 9
    pacificism, 199

Time
    wasting of, 77

Transference, 251

Transformation
    God found in, 20

Truth
    applied, 124
    broadcasting, 39
    concept of the Absolute, 37
    finding and hearing, 121

Truth (continued)
    immortality in, 71
    lasting success in, 32
    rejection of, 54
    renewal of, 278

### -U-

Unconscious
    cornerstone, 187
    formation of, 12
    formation of the, 28
    healing with awareness, 31
Uniqueness
    finding, 62
Unitarian Church
    rebelliousness, 111
Unity, 147, 148, 261
    finding, 178, 202

### -V-

Vatican
    knowledge concealed, 123
Violence, 244
Virgin Mary
    worship, 247
Visualization
    progress through, 95

### -W-

Waste
    teachings on, 115
Wealth, 239
    key to, 242
    poverty consciousness, 96
    protection of, 181
    purpose of, 240
    real, 213
Welfare, 240

Women
    New Age, 276
Words
    renewal of, 278
Work
    seen as pain, 173
World War II, 199
    reincarnations post, 98
Worldliness, 170, 212
    real wealth, 213
    teachings on, 114

### -Y-

Yuppiedom, 196, 207

# ABOUT THE AUTHOR

For over forty years, Reverend Dr. Albert Gani (1943-2018), through faith and seeking the presence of God, helped people find purpose and meaning in their lives, motivating them towards the pursuit of happiness through ethics and faith.

His work took him from coast to coast in the United States, as well as Europe and Mexico. He authored over thirty books, wrote numerous articles, and lectured extensively. Throughout his life, he motivated people and organizations to effect major changes through the application of spiritual and ethical principles.

A true Renaissance man, he brought to his teachings a keen wit, a versatile knowledge of world history and politics, proficiency in languages, and great knowledge of music and philosophy. In this way, he challenged, entertained, and provoked people to rethink and restructure their lives.

He used his own crises and struggles as examples in his teachings. Perhaps most apparent and inspiring of all of his qualities was his courageous, ethical, and loving stance for the truth, regardless of the outcome.

Books by Reverend Dr. Albert Gani available at:
www.churchofthepath.org

www.ingramcontent.com/pod-product-compliance
Lightning Source LLC
Chambersburg PA
CBHW062152080426
42734CB00010B/1659